New Mother's Cookbook

Exeter Books

NEW YORK

Introduction

Introduction

New Mother's Cookbook by Donna Paananen is designed to fill the needs of the busy mother—whether she is a full-time homemaker or working outside the home.

The approach to this book is basic and simple—sound nutrition and sensible eating habits incorporated into a balanced diet. Emphasis has been given to recipes which supply the daily nutritional needs of mother, baby and the rest of the family. Armed with the basics of good nutrition as outlined in Nutrition Facts, the new mother or father will be able to build menus to suit their tastes and meet dietary requirements.

Many of the dishes—especially the casseroles—can be frozen, making meal preparation easier the first weeks mother and baby are home from the hospital.

For those luxurious quiet moments when mom and dad are alone, we have included a chapter of recipes just for two. All you need do is add candlelight.

And, the chapter on baby and toddler foods will stimulate your imagination when the time comes for baby to join the family at mealtime.

We wish you the very best with your new baby and are confident that this cookbook will make mealtime a pleasant experience for the entire family.

ISBN 0-89673-111-1
Copyright © MCMLXXXI by Donna Paananen
All rights reserved.
Published by American Baby Books
Printed and bound in U.S.A.
This edition published by Exeter Books,
By arrangement with American Baby Books.
Exeter 1981 Edition
Exeter is a trademark of Simon & Schuster.
Distributed by Bookthrift
New York, New York

Contents

Contents

NUTRITION FACTS

Good nutrition and sound eating habits are always important to good health, but never more so than during pregnancy and lactation. By preparing well-planned meals you help yourself, your baby, and the rest of the family.

Since the growing fetus is exposed to whatever the mother ingests, it is important to follow the doctor's advice regarding diet, especially if you are on a sodium-restricted diet. (You will notice that the recipes in this book call for salt as an optional ingredient and should be used with discretion.)

Generally speaking, there are certain items which should be avoided entirely during pregnancy and lactation: alcohol, coffee, tea and herbal teas, chocolate, soft drinks, nicotine, artificial sweeteners, and drugs taken without your doctor's consent—even such over-the-counter drugs as aspirin, laxatives, unprescribed vitamins, and cold or sinus medications.

Diet During Pregnancy

An appropriate diet during pregnancy has three essential components: 1) 1 gram of protein per 2.2 pounds body weight, plus 30 grams; 20 grams if lactating, 2) essential vitamins and minerals, especially calcium and iron, and 3) 2300 to 2500 calories per day.

Pregnancy is no time to diet. The reduction of calories required by diets also means a reduction in necessary nutrients.

Choose foods from the four basic food groups and include these in your daily menu, observing the number of servings required. See the chart below for the dietary recommendations.

Vegetables and Fruits

Fresh produce is preferable to frozen or canned, since prepared foods often contain flavor enhancers such as salt and sugar. Include a variety of vegetables and fruits to provide several nutrients. Dried fruits contain vitamin B and iron, and nuts are a great source of protein.

Milk and Cheese

Milk contains protein, calcium, phosphorous, and vitamins A and D. Three servings a day are required and can be obtained from such foods as cottage cheese, Swiss or Cheddar cheese, and yogurt. If you prefer flavored yogurt, it is best to buy the unflavored form and add your own flavorings, such as fresh fruit, since commercially flavored yogurt is often sweetened with sugar.

Another food included in this group is egg—considered to be the perfect source of protein. Eaten in a sensible, balanced diet, eggs do not cause excess cholesterol.

Butter and margarine are included in this group. When deciding which to use, remember that margarine is more easily digested.

Breads and Cereals

When thinking of good nutrition, think whole grain. Breads made of whole wheat flour are far more nutritious than those made with bleached, white flour. Whole grain cereals not only make good breakfasts, but good snacks. They are a good source of roughage and some B vitamins.

When buying rice, choose brown and noninstant varieties.

Meat and Poultry

All cuts of meat are fairly equal in terms of nutrition. Fish and poultry, however, tend to have less fat. Canned salmon and tuna contain a high content of vitamins B and D.

Daily Dietary Recommendations During Pregnancy and Lactation

The following recommendations supply the basic nutrients needed during pregnancy but usually not enough calories to produce the suggested weight gain. Many women will need more food from these food groups to meet their caloric needs.

Minimum Daily Servings

Food Group	Pregnancy	Breast-feeding
Milk/Cheese	3 servings (5 for teenagers)	4 servings (6 for teenagers)
Vegetable/Fruit	6 servings	6 servings
Vitamin A source	1 daily	1 daily
Vitamin C source	1 daily	1 daily
Dark green, leafy	1 daily	1 daily
Fiber source	1 daily	1 daily
Bread/Cereal	6 servings	6 servings
Meat/Poultry/Fish Egg/Bean	2 servings	2 servings

Adapted from "Food While You're Pregnant,"
Michigan Department of Public Health, Lansing, Michigan

Principal Nutrients Required Daily

Good Sources

Proteins
Eggs, milk, soy, whole grains, animal and fish meat, dairy products
Incomplete proteins can be combined to give complete protein, e.g., grains/milk/legumes **or** fresh greens/rice **or** peas/sesame seeds **or** peanut butter/bread/milk

Fats
Butter, margarine, cooking fats and oils, salad oils and dressings, fat meats

Carbohydrates
Starches: breads, cereals, corn, potatoes, rice, noodles, spaghetti
Sugars: honey, molasses, syrups, jellies
Fruits: dried, sweetened, fresh (smaller amount)

Vitamin A
Dark green and deep yellow vegetables, apricots, cantaloupe, butter, fortified margarine, whole milk, Cheddar cheese, liver, kidney, eggs

Vitamin B₁ (Thiamin)
Lean meats, fish, poultry, liver, milk, pork, dried yeast, whole grain cereals, enriched breads and cereals

Vitamin B₂ (Riboflavin)
Eggs, enriched breads and cereals, leafy green vegetables, liver, lean meats, dried yeast, milk

Vitamin B₆
Wheat germ, vegetables, meat, dried yeast, whole grain cereals

Vitamin B₁₂
Liver, kidney, milk, oysters, saltwater fish, lean meat

Folic Acid
Leafy green vegetables, food yeast, meats

Niacin
Lean meats, liver, dried enriched breads, cereals, eggs

Vitamin C (Ascorbic Acid)
Citrus fruits, berries, cantaloupe, broccoli, green and sweet red peppers, raw cabbage, Brussels sprouts, potatoes cooked in their jackets

Vitamin D
Fish liver oils, Vitamin D fortified milk, egg yolks, salmon, tuna

Vitamin E
Vegetable oils, whole grain cereals, wheat germ, lettuce

Vitamin K
Pork liver, cabbage, cauliflower, soybeans

Calcium
Milk (all types), cheese, ice cream, green leafy vegetables, e.g., collards, kale, mustard greens, turnips or broccoli

Iron
Lean meats, liver, heart, oysters, egg yolks, dark green leafy vegetables, dried fruits, whole grain and enriched breads, cereals, molasses

Iodine
Saltwater fish, shellfish, iodized salt

Other minerals
Widely distributed throughout food, they usually present no problem of nutritional deficiency

Adapted from "Beginning Together," courtesy of the
Childbirth Education Association, Milwaukee, Wisconsin.

BREAKFASTS

Breads and cereals provide energy, vitamins, minerals, and a small amount of protein in the daily diet. By making your own breads and cereals, you avoid commercial additives and can include nutritious ingredients that you choose yourself.

Bran Muffins

Makes 1 dozen.

- 1 egg
- ¾ cup milk
- ⅓ cup honey
- 2 tablespoons vegetable oil
- 1 cup whole wheat flour
- 1¼ cups bran
- ¼ cup raw wheat germ
- ½ teaspoon salt
- 1 teaspoon baking soda
- 1 teaspoon baking powder
- ½ cup raisins or currants

Preheat oven to 400°. Combine egg, milk, honey and oil; mix well. Combine remaining ingredients; mix well. Make a well in the center of the dry ingredients. Pour milk mixture into well; stir until just moistened. Spoon into well-greased muffin cups. Bake 20 minutes, or until golden.

Dropped Baking Powder Biscuits

Makes 2 dozen.

- 1¾ cups whole wheat flour
- ¾ teaspoon salt
- 2½ teaspoons baking powder
- 5 tablespoons butter or margarine, chilled
- 1 cup milk or buttermilk

Preheat oven to 425°. Combine flour, salt and baking powder in a medium bowl. Cut in butter with a pastry blender until mixture is crumbly. Make a well in the center and add milk. Stir until all ingredients are thoroughly blended. Drop by teaspoonfuls onto an ungreased baking sheet. Bake 12 to 15 minutes.

Cranberry-Orange Bread

Makes 1 loaf.

- 2 cups unbleached flour, sifted
- 1 cup granulated sugar
- 1½ teaspoons baking powder
- ½ teaspoon baking soda
- 1 teaspoon salt
- 2 tablespoons melted shortening
- ½ teaspoon grated lemon rind
- 1 teaspoon grated orange rind
- ¾ cup orange juice
- 1 egg, beaten
- 1 cup chopped nuts
- 1 pound cranberries

Sift together dry ingredients in a large bowl. Add shortening, lemon and orange rinds, orange juice and egg. Mix until just blended. Fold in nuts and berries. Pour into a greased 9 x 5-inch loaf pan. (Press into corners, leaving a slight hollow in the center.) Set aside for 20 minutes. Preheat oven to 350°. Bake bread 60 to 70 minutes or until wooden pick inserted into center comes out clean. Cool on a wire rack 10 minutes before removing from pan. Cool completely. Store in refrigerator.

Quick Fiber Bread

Makes 1 loaf.

- 1 cup whole wheat flour
- 1 cup unbleached flour
- 1¼ cups bran
- 1 cup raw wheat germ
- 1½ teaspoons baking powder
- 1 teaspoon baking soda
- 1 teaspoon salt
- 5 tablespoons brown sugar
- 3 tablespoons margarine or shortening
- 1 cup buttermilk or soured milk

Preheat oven to 375°. Grease an 8-or 9-inch round cake pan. Combine dry ingredients; mix thoroughly. Cut in margarine until well blended. Make a well in the center of the flour mixture. Pour in buttermilk; mix well. Form dough into a round loaf. Place in prepared pan. Cut a cross in the top of the loaf. Bake 35 to 40 minutes or until a toothpick inserted in center comes out clean.

Cranberry-Orange Bread

Dilly Casserole Bread

Makes 1 loaf.

- 1 package active dry yeast
- ¼ cup warm water (105° to 115°)
- 1 cup creamed cottage cheese
- 1 tablespoon melted margarine
- 2 tablespoons sugar
- 1 teaspoon salt
- ¼ teaspoon baking soda
- 1 tablespoon minced onion
- 2 teaspoons dillseed
- 1 egg, beaten
- 2¼ to 2½ cups unbleached flour

Dissolve yeast in water; set aside 10 minutes. Heat cottage cheese to lukewarm. Place margarine, sugar, salt, soda, onion and dillseed in a large bowl. Beat in egg. Add yeast mixture and mix well. Add flour gradually, beating well after each addition. Cover and let rise in a warm place until doubled in bulk, about 1 hour. Stir dough down. (It will be sticky.) Turn into a well-greased 1½-quart casserole. Cover and let rise until doubled in bulk. Preheat oven to 350°. Brush top with butter, if desired. Bake bread 35 to 45 minutes or until crust is golden. Cool 10 minutes on wire rack before removing from casserole.

Steamed Brown Bread

Makes 2 loaves.

- ¾ cup molasses
- 2 cups buttermilk or yogurt
- 1½ teaspoons baking soda
- 1 teaspoon salt
- 1 cup cornmeal
- 1 cup white or rye flour
- 1 cup whole wheat flour
- 1 cup raisins

Combine molasses and buttermilk; mix well and set aside. Combine dry ingredients in a large mixing bowl. Add milk mixture, a small amount at a time, stirring after each addition. Stir until all ingredients are just moistened. Fold in raisins. Spoon batter into 2 well-greased 1-pound coffee cans or 1 2-pound coffee can. Cover with foil. Secure foil with string. Place cans on metal rack in bottom of a slow cooker or Dutch oven. Pour at least 2 cups of boiling water into pot. Cover and cook on high in a slow cooker or on low on top of stove. Cook 2½ to 3 hours for small cans, 3½ to 4 hours for the large can or until a toothpick inserted in center comes out clean. Remove cans from pot and cool 5 to 10 minutes. Turn bread out onto a cooling rack. Serve warm.

Carrot-Honey Bread

Makes 1 loaf.

- 3 eggs
- ⅔ cup honey
- ½ cup vegetable oil
- 1 cup unbleached flour
- 1¼ cups whole wheat flour
- 1 tablespoon baking powder
- 1 teaspoon salt
- ¼ teaspoon ginger
- 1½ teaspoons cinnamon
- 1 cup rolled oats
- 2 cups grated carrots
- ⅔ cup chopped nuts, optional

Preheat oven to 325°. Beat together eggs, honey and oil. Set aside. Combine remaining ingredients, except carrots and nuts. Stir egg mixture into dry ingredients until just moistened. Fold in carrots and nuts. Spoon batter into a greased 9 x 5-inch loaf pan. Bake 1¼ hours or until a toothpick inserted in center comes out clean. Cool on wire rack 10 minutes; turn out and cool thoroughly.

Potato Rolls

Makes 3 dozen.

- 1½ cups warm water (105° to 115°)
- 2 packages active dry yeast
- ¼ cup honey
- 2 teaspoons salt
- 2 eggs
- ½ cup margarine, softened
- ½ cup unseasoned, warm mashed potatoes
- 6½ cups unbleached flour or part whole wheat flour
- 3 tablespoons melted butter or margarine
- Poppy or sesame seeds

Pour warm water into a large mixing bowl; sprinkle yeast over. Stir in honey and salt until mixture is blended. Set aside until mixture is bubbly. Add eggs, margarine, potatoes and 3 cups of the flour. Mix with electric mixer until smooth. Gradually add 2 cups flour, beating with wooden spoon until thoroughly blended. Add remaining flour by kneading until dough is smooth and leaves the sides of the bowl. Brush top of dough with 1 tablespoon of the melted butter. Cover and let rise in refrigerator for about 2 hours or until doubled in bulk. Punch down. Shape into cloverleaf, Parker House or hamburger rolls. Brush with remaining butter and sprinkle on seeds. Cover and let rise 1 hour in a warm place. Preheat oven to 400°. Bake rolls about 12 minutes or until golden.

Sunflower Seed Muffins

Makes 1 dozen.

⅓ cup honey
¼ cup vegetable oil
½ cup milk
1 egg, beaten
¼ teaspoon grated lemon peel
1 cup whole wheat flour
½ cup unbleached flour
½ cup raw sunflower seeds
½ teaspoon salt
2 teaspoons baking powder

Preheat oven to 375°. Combine honey, oil, milk, egg and lemon peel. Mix together remaining ingredients in a large bowl. Make a well in the center. Pour milk mixture into well and stir until just moistened. (Batter will be lumpy.) Fill greased muffin tins ⅓ full. Bake 20 minutes or until golden. Cool on wire racks.

Whole Wheat French Bread

Makes 2 loaves.

2 packages active dry yeast
1¾ cups lukewarm water
3 tablespoons honey
1½ tablespoons vegetable oil
2 teaspoons salt
1½ cups all-purpose flour
3 cups whole wheat flour
1 cup unbleached flour (approximately)

Dissolve yeast in water in a large mixing bowl. Stir in remaining ingredients, except flour, mixing well. Add flour to make a soft dough. Cover and let rise in a warm place (80° to 85° F.) for 1 to 2 hours or until doubled in bulk. Turn dough out onto a heavily floured surface and knead until smooth, about 10 minutes. Shape into 2 long French loaves. Place loaves on a greased baking sheet. Cut about ¼-inch deep diagonal slits into the top of the loaves. Cover and let rise until almost doubled in bulk. Preheat oven to 400°. Pour boiling water into a cake pan to ½ inch deep. Place on bottom shelf of oven. Bake loaves 15 minutes. Reduce heat to 350° and bake approximately 30 minutes longer.

Pumpkin Bread

Makes 3 loaves.

3½ cups whole wheat flour
¼ cup raw wheat germ
½ teaspoon baking powder
2 teaspoons baking soda
1 teaspoon salt
1¼ teaspoons cinnamon
1 teaspoon ground cloves
¾ cup shortening
2 cups firmly packed brown sugar
4 eggs
2 cups canned pumpkin
⅔ cup water
¾ cup raisins or chopped dates
⅔ cup chopped nuts

Preheat oven to 350°. In a mixing bowl, stir together flour, wheat germ, baking powder, soda, salt, cinnamon and cloves. Set aside. Cream shortening with sugar. Beat in eggs until light and fluffy. Stir in pumpkin and water. Gradually add flour mixture; mix well. Fold in raisins and nuts. Pour into 3 well-greased 9 x 5-inch loaf pans. Bake for 1 hour or until a toothpick inserted in center comes out clean. Cool 10 minutes on a wire rack. Remove from pans; cool.

Scones

Makes 1 dozen.

2 cups unbleached flour
2 teaspoons baking powder
¼ teaspoon salt
¼ cup butter or margarine
⅔ cup milk
⅓ cup raisins

Preheat oven to 400°. Sift together flour, baking powder and salt. Cut in butter with a pastry blender until mixture resembles crumbs. Add milk and raisins; mix to a soft dough. Turn onto a lightly floured surface. Knead dough gently. Roll out ½ inch thick. Cut into rounds with a 2-inch floured biscuit cutter. Place on a greased baking sheet. Bake 10 to 12 minutes or until golden.

Yorkshire Cheese Biscuits

Makes 1 dozen.

1 egg
⅔ cup milk
1 cup grated sharp Cheddar cheese
2⅔ cups whole wheat flour
1 teaspoon baking powder
¼ teaspoon salt

Preheat oven to 400°. Mix egg and milk together; set aside. Combine remaining ingredients; mix well. Make a well in the middle of the flour mixture; gradually add egg mixture, stirring well after each addition. Beat until a soft dough forms. Form into a ball; turn out onto a well-floured surface. Roll ½ inch thick. Cut into rounds with a 2-inch floured biscuit cutter. Place on a greased baking sheet. Bake 10 minutes.

High Protein Pancakes

Makes 18.

    3 eggs, separated
    ¾ cup cottage cheese
    ¼ teaspoon salt
    1¼ cups whole wheat flour
    ⅓ cup non-instant powdered
       milk
    ¼ cup raw wheat germ
    ¼ cup milk or buttermilk

Place egg yolks, cottage cheese, salt, flour and powdered milk in a blender or food processor. Blend until smooth. Blend in wheat germ and milk. Beat egg whites until soft peaks are formed. Fold into cottage cheese mixture. Lightly butter a griddle and heat. Drop batter by tablespoonfuls onto griddle. Cook until brown on 1 side. Turn and brown the other side.

Note: Pancakes can be made without separating the eggs. Simply beat the ingredients until smooth.

Granola Muffins

Makes 1 dozen.

    1¼ cups Granola (Recipe on
       page 13)
    ¼ cup raw wheat germ
    1 cup whole wheat flour
    ½ cup raisins
    ½ teaspoon salt
    1 teaspoon baking soda
    1 teaspoon baking powder
    ¾ cup milk
    ⅓ cup honey
    2 tablespoons vegetable oil
    1 egg, beaten

Preheat oven to 400°. Combine dry ingredients and set aside. Combine milk, honey, oil and egg, mixing thoroughly. Add to dry ingredients; stir until just moistened. Spoon into well-greased muffin cups. Bake 15 minutes, or until golden.

Blueberry Muffins

Makes 12 muffins.

    1 cup packed brown sugar
    ½ cup shortening
    2 eggs
    1 teaspoon baking soda
    ½ cup sour milk
    ½ teaspoon salt
    2½ cups sifted flour
    1 pint blueberries

Combine sugar and shortening in a mixing bowl; cream until light and fluffy. Add eggs, one at a time, beating well after each addition. Combine baking soda and sour milk; set aside. Combine salt and 2 cups of the flour; mix lightly. Alternately add milk and flour to mixing bowl, beating well after each addition. Combine remaining flour with blueberries; mix well. Fold blueberries into batter. Pour into greased muffin tins. Bake at 350° for 25 minutes, until golden brown.

Rye Pancakes

Makes 16.

    1 cup rye flour
    ¾ teaspoon salt
    2 teaspoons baking powder
    ¼ cup non-instant, non-fat dry
       milk
    ½ cup raw wheat germ
    1½ cups milk
    2 tablespoons vegetable oil
    2 eggs, separated

Sift together flour, salt, baking powder and dry milk. Stir in wheat germ. Combine milk, oil and egg yolks, beating well. Add to dry ingredients and stir gently. Beat egg whites until stiff but not dry. Fold into batter. Pour by spoonfuls onto a lightly-greased, hot griddle.

Eggs and Muffins

Makes 4 servings.

    ½ cup milk
    1 tablespoon flour
    1 teaspoon salt, optional
    4 slices Swiss cheese
    ¼ cup dry sherry
    4 slices Canadian bacon, fried
    4 eggs, poached
    2 English muffins, split and
       toasted

Combine milk and flour and mix until well blended. Pour into a small saucepan. Add salt and cheese. Cook over low heat, stirring constantly, until smooth and thickened. Remove from heat and add sherry. Place a piece of Canadian bacon on top of each muffin half. Top each with an egg. Spoon sauce over top.

Slightly undercook pancakes; then warm leftovers in the toaster or under the broiler when needed.

Cheese Pancakes

Makes 18.

    2 cups whole wheat flour
    2 teaspoons baking powder
    1 egg
    1¼ cups milk
    ½ cup grated Cheddar cheese

Combine dry ingredients and mix lightly. In a separate bowl beat egg until frothy. Gradually add milk and blend well. Add cheese and mix well. Stir into dry ingredients; mixing well. Ladle onto hot grill and cook until browned. Turn and cook remaining side.

Wheatless Banana Bread

Makes 2 loaves.

    3 cups soy flour
    1 cup corn flour*
2½ teaspoons baking soda
    1 teaspoon salt
    ½ cup soy oil
1½ cups granulated sugar
    1 egg
    ½ cup milk
    8 medium bananas, mashed
    ⅔ cup slivered almonds

Line 2 9 x 5-inch loaf pans with waxed paper. Grease thoroughly. Sift together soy flour, corn flour, baking soda and salt. Set aside. Combine oil and sugar in a mixing bowl; mix well. Beat in egg. Alternately stir in flour mixture and milk. Add bananas and mix well. Stir in almonds. Pour into prepared pans. Heat oven at 250° for 5 minutes. Turn off heat. Place pans in oven for 45 minutes. Set oven at 350°. Bake bread for 30 minutes or until golden brown. Remove from oven. Cool in pans.

*Available at health food stores.

Wheat Germ Biscuits

Makes 1 dozen.

    ½ cup chopped currants or raisins
    2 eggs, lightly beaten
    ⅓ cup buttermilk or soured milk
    1 cup unbleached flour
    1 cup whole wheat flour
    ¼ cup packed brown sugar
    1 tablespoon baking powder
    1 teaspoon salt
    ½ teaspoon baking soda
    4 tablespoons margarine or butter
    2 cups raw wheat germ

Combine currants, eggs and buttermilk; mix well and set aside. Combine the flours, brown sugar, baking powder, salt and baking soda. Cut in margarine with a pastry blender or fork until mixture resembles coarse crumbs. Preheat oven to 400°. Stir in wheat germ. Make a well in the mixture. Pour liquid mixture into well; mix thoroughly. Gather into a ball. Turn out onto a lightly floured surface. Knead lightly 5 or 6 times. Roll out and cut into 2-inch rounds. Place on greased baking sheet. Bake 12 to 15 minutes.

Alternate method: Divide dough in two. Roll out each part into a large circle ½ inch thick. Cut each circle into 6 wedges.

Salt-Free Bread

Makes 4 loaves.

    4 cups warm water
    ⅔ cup molasses
1½ tablespoons granulated sugar
    1 tablespoon salt substitute
    2 packages active dry yeast dissolved in ½ cup warm water (105° to 115°)
    5 tablespoons vegetable oil
    ⅔ cup instant whole wheat cereal
    1 cup raw wheat germ
  13 cups unbleached flour or a mixture of unbleached and whole wheat
    ¼ to ½ cup cornmeal

Combine the first 6 ingredients in a very large bowl. Add wheat cereal and wheat germ; mix well. Gradually stir in flour. Turn out onto a well-floured board and knead for about 10 minutes or until dough is smooth and elastic. Knead in cornmeal. Place dough in a lightly-greased bowl; turn to grease top. Cover with a damp towel. Let rise in a warm place for 2 hours or until doubled in bulk. Punch down. Divide into 4 pieces. Shape into loaves. Place in greased 9 x 5-inch loaf pans. Cover with a damp towel and let rise for 30 minutes or until almost doubled in bulk. Preheat oven to 375°. Bake bread for 40 to 45 minutes or until golden. Brush tops with melted salt-free butter, if desired. Cool on wire racks.

Anadama Bread

Makes 2 loaves.

    2 packages active dry yeast
    ½ cup warm water (105° to 115°)
1½ cups cornmeal
    ⅓ cup old-fashioned molasses
    ¼ cup butter or margarine
    2 teaspoons salt
    2 cups hot water (125°)
    ¼ cup raw wheat germ
    4 cups (approximately) unbleached flour or a combination of unbleached flour and whole wheat flour
    2 eggs

Dissolve yeast in warm water in a mixing bowl. With mixer at low speed, add cornmeal, molasses, butter, salt, hot water, wheat germ and two cups of the flour. Beat 2 minutes at medium speed, scraping bowl often. Add eggs and beat 2 minutes. Add remaining flour by hand, forming a soft dough. Turn out on a lightly floured surface. Knead in enough flour until dough is no longer sticky. Knead until smooth and elastic, about 10 minutes. Place in a greased bowl, turning to grease all sides. Cover and let rise in a warm place for 1 hour or until doubled in bulk.

Punch down and shape into two loaves. Place in two well-greased 1-pound coffee cans or 8 x 4-inch loaf pans. Cover and let rise in a warm place 45 minutes or until almost doubled in bulk. Preheat oven to 375°. Bake 35 to 40 minutes or until tops are browned and loaves sound hollow when tapped. Turn loaves out onto wire racks to cool.

Rhubarb Bread

Makes 2 loaves.

- 4 tablespoons brown sugar
- 1 tablespoon raw wheat germ
- 5 tablespoons whole wheat flour
- 4 tablespoons margarine
- 1 cup packed brown sugar
- ⅔ cup vegetable oil
- 1 egg
- 1 cup sour milk
- 1 teaspoon salt
- 1 teaspoon baking soda
- 1 teaspoon vanilla
- 1½ cups whole wheat flour
- ½ cup raw wheat germ
- ½ cup soy flour
- 1½ cups diced rhubarb
- ½ cup chopped nuts

Preheat oven to 350°. Combine the first 3 ingredients in a mixing bowl. Cut in margarine until crumbly. Set aside. Combine the 1 cup brown sugar, oil and egg. Add milk; mix well. Stir in salt, soda and vanilla. Add whole wheat flour, ½ cup wheat germ and soy flour. Fold in rhubarb. Pour batter into 2 well-greased 8 x 5-inch loaf pans. Sprinkle nuts over top. Sprinkle reserved brown sugar mixture over top. Bake 1 hour or until top springs back when touched lightly.

Granola

Makes approximately 11 cups.

- 4 cups rolled oats or a mixture of rolled grains
- 2 cups whole wheat flour
- 1 cup raw wheat germ
- 1 cup bran flakes
- ¾ cup soy flour
- 1 tablespoon nutritional yeast
- 1 teaspoon salt
- ⅓ cup hot water
- ½ cup honey
- ⅔ cup vegetable oil
- 1 cup chopped nuts
- 1 cup raisins

Preheat oven to 275°. Combine the dry ingredients, except nuts and raisins, in a large bowl. Mix together water, honey and vegetable oil. Stir into dry ingredients. Mix well. Stir in nuts. Spread mixture very thinly on 2 baking sheets. Bake 45 minutes or until crisp and golden, stirring occasionally. Add raisins and mix lightly. Cool completely. Store in a large container. Serve with milk, yogurt or additional fruit, nuts or seeds.

High-Protein Granola

Makes 6 cups.

- 5 cups rolled oats
- ½ cup raw wheat germ
- ½ cup bran flakes
- ½ cup nonfat dry milk powder
- ¼ cup raw sunflower or sesame seeds
- ¼ cup almonds or walnuts
- ¼ cup sifted soy flour
- 1 egg
- ½ cup vegetable oil
- ½ cup honey
- 1 teaspoon vanilla
- ½ cup raisins

Preheat oven to 225°. Combine all dry ingredients, except raisins, in a very large mixing bowl. In a separate bowl, beat egg until foamy. Add oil, honey and vanilla; mix well. Combine dry and liquid ingredients; mix well. Spread mixture on a large baking sheet. Bake for 1 hour, stirring occasionally. Remove from oven. Stir in raisins. Cool on baking sheets. Store in tightly sealed containers.

For variety, bake bread in cleaned, greased, one-pound coffee cans, or form round loaves and bake on greased baking sheets.

Pruneola

Makes approximately 4 cups.

- ¼ cup vegetable oil
- 2 tablespoons honey
- 3 cups combination of rolled oats, rolled wheat, and/or rolled rye
- 2 tablespoons soy flour
- ½ cup raw wheat germ
- ½ cup bran flakes
- 2 tablespoons sesame seeds
- ½ cup raw sunflower seeds
- ¾ cup chopped prunes

Preheat oven to 300°. Combine oil and honey in a heavy saucepan; heat until honey is melted. Combine remaining ingredients, except prunes, in a large bowl. Stir honey mixture into dry ingredients. Spread mixture very thinly on 2 large baking sheets. Bake, stirring occasionally, for 25 minutes or until mixture is golden. Pour into a large bowl. Immediately stir in prunes; cool. Store in a large, tightly covered container. Eat as a cereal with milk or yogurt.

LUNCH FARE

This chapter includes endless possibilities for making your midday meal a healthy interlude in a busy day. Included are recipes for delicious soups and sandwiches, which combined with a salad, create a well-balanced meal. Quiches, hearty omelets and casseroles include several food groups in a single dish. So, instead of grabbing a quick bite, make lunchtime count in a total, healthy diet.

Minestrone

Makes 8 servings.

1½ cups dried Great Northern
    or navy beans
  6 cups water
  8 slices bacon, chopped
  2 tablespoons vegetable oil
  1 cup chopped onion
  2 cloves garlic, minced
  1 cup chopped celery
  2 cups sliced carrots
  3 cups chopped tomatoes
  1 to 2 cups fresh green beans,
    halved
  ¾ teaspoon dried oregano
  1 teaspoon thyme
  ¼ teaspoon sweet basil
  1 bay leaf
  2 to 3 cups cooked macaroni
    Salt to taste, optional
  ¼ teaspoon black pepper
    Minced parsley, grated
    Parmesan cheese, optional

Soak dried beans in water overnight. Place beans, water and bacon in a large soup kettle or Dutch oven. Bring to a boil. Reduce heat and simmer, covered, approximately 2 hours or until beans are tender. Stir during cooking to be sure there is enough liquid. Add more water, if necessary. Remove from heat and set aside. Heat oil in a frying pan. Sauté onion, garlic, celery and carrots until vegetables are tender, about 15 minutes. Stir in tomato, green beans and herbs. Simmer, covered, about 15 minutes. Stir in navy beans and liquid, macaroni, salt and pepper. Bring to a boil. Cover and reduce heat. Simmer 30 to 35 minutes, stirring several times. Discard bay leaf. Serve, garnished with parsley and Parmesan cheese.

Clam and Vegetable Stew

Makes 4 to 6 servings.

  2 carrots, pared and diced
  1 cup frozen peas
  3 small new potatoes, pared
    and diced
  3 small white onions, peeled
  2 ribs celery, sliced
  1 8¾-ounce can cream-style
    corn
  1 bay leaf
  ⅛ teaspoon crushed sweet basil
  ⅛ teaspoon rosemary
  ⅛ teaspoon crushed thyme
  1 10½-ounce can clam juice
  2 8-ounce cans minced clams
  ½ cup butter

Place vegetables, herbs and clam juice in a soup kettle or Dutch oven. Add water to barely cover vegetables. Bring to a boil. Reduce heat, cover and simmer for 30 minutes, or until vegetables are tender. Discard bay leaf. Add clams and butter; heat until butter melts. Serve with toasted bread rounds, if desired.

Watercress Soup

Makes 3 to 4 servings.

  2 tablespoons butter or
    margarine
  1 cup chopped potato
  1 cup chopped onion
  1 bunch watercress, chopped
  2 cups chicken or beef broth
    Salt, optional
    Freshly ground black pepper
  ⅛ teaspoon nutmeg

Heat butter in a large skillet. Add potato and onion and sauté 2 to 3 minutes. Add watercress and sauté 2 minutes, stirring frequently. Add broth, salt, pepper and nutmeg. Cover and simmer until potato is tender, 15 to 20 minutes. Serve as is or puree in a blender or food processor. Serve garnished with croutons, if desired.

LUNCH FARE

Ground Beef and Vegetable Soup

Makes 5 to 6 servings.

- 1 pound ground beef
- 1 cup chopped onion
- 1 cup sliced carrots
- ½ cup diced celery
- 1 cup diced potato
- ½ cup shredded cabbage
- 2½ cups chopped tomatoes
- 4 cups water
- 1 small bay leaf
- ½ teaspoon minced fresh sweet basil, or ¼ teaspoon dried
- ½ teaspoon dried thyme
- ½ teaspoon black pepper
  Salt to taste, optional
  Grated Parmesan cheese
  Minced parsley

Place ground beef and onion in a large saucepan or Dutch oven. Sauté until onion is tender. (Add a small amount of vegetable oil if beef is very lean.) Add vegetables, water and seasonings. Bring to a boil. Reduce heat, cover and simmer for 1 hour or until vegetables are tender. Garnish with Parmesan cheese and parsley.

Split Pea Soup

Makes 4 servings.

- 2 cups dried split peas, sorted and rinsed
- 1 or 2 meaty ham bones
- 6 cups water or half water, half chicken broth
- 1 cup chopped celery
- 1 cup chopped carrots
- 1 cup chopped onion
- ¼ teaspoon thyme
- 1 bay leaf
- ⅛ teaspoon ground cloves
  Salt, optional
  Freshly ground black pepper

Place peas and ham bones in a large soup kettle. Add water or broth. Bring to a boil. Reduce heat and simmer 2 minutes. Remove from heat, cover, and let stand 1 hour. Add remaining ingredients. Simmer, covered, 2 to 3 hours or until peas are tender. Remove ham bones and cut meat into bite-sized pieces. Return meat to soup.

Golden Harvest Soup

Makes 10 to 12 servings.

- Ham or beef soup bones
- 2 cups lentils, sorted and rinsed
- 2 quarts beef broth, or water
- 1 cup chopped onion
- 1 clove garlic, minced
- 2 bay leaves
- 2 cups sliced carrots
- 2 cups chopped tomatoes
- 2 cups cubed eggplant
- 2 cups shredded cabbage
- 2 cups cubed zucchini or yellow summer squash
- 1 cup bean sprouts
- ¼ cup soy sauce
- 2 teaspoons minced sweet basil
- ¼ cup chopped parsley
  Salt, optional
  Freshly ground black pepper

Place soup bones, lentils and broth in a soup kettle. Bring to a boil, reduce heat and skim. Remove from heat and let stand for 1 hour. Add onion, garlic, bay leaves, carrots and tomatoes and simmer 1½ hours, or until lentils are tender. Remove soup bones. Add eggplant, cabbage, zucchini and bean sprouts. Return to a simmer. Add soy sauce, basil, parsley, salt and pepper. Simmer 5 minutes. Discard bay leaves.

Chicken and Noodle Soup

Makes 4 to 6 servings.

- 3 to 4 pounds chicken, cut up
- ½ cup sliced onion
- 1 celery rib with leaves, chopped
- 2 carrots, sliced
- 1 sprig parsley
- 1½ teaspoons salt, optional
- ½ teaspoon black pepper
- 2 cloves garlic, optional
  Homemade Noodles

Wash chicken and pat dry. Place in a large, heavy kettle along with giblets. Add just enough water to cover. Add remaining ingredients. Heat to boiling; reduce heat and cover. Simmer about 45 minutes or until chicken is tender. Remove chicken and strain broth. Discard skin and bones. Bring broth to a boil and drop in noodles. Reduce heat; cover and simmer 15 minutes. Add chicken and heat another 5 minutes.

Homemade Noodles

- 1 egg, beaten
- ½ teaspoon salt, optional
- 2 tablespoons milk
- 1 cup flour

Combine egg, salt and milk. Stir in flour; dough will be stiff. Roll out very thin on floured board. Dry 30 minutes. Roll up dough and slice as desired. Spread out noodles to dry. Dry at least 2 hours.

If you are on a sodium-restricted diet, omit the salt in the recipes. Add a little minced garlic or finely minced chives in place of salt.

Winter Stew

Makes 6 servings.

1¾ cups dried lentils, sorted, washed and drained
6 cups chicken or beef broth
2 cups chopped green onion
1 cup chopped celery
2 cups chopped carrots
1½ cups cubed ham
3 cloves garlic, chopped
⅓ cup chopped parsley
½ teaspoon thyme
1 bay leaf
Freshly ground black pepper
Minced parsley, chopped hard-boiled eggs, or sour cream, optional

Place lentils and broth in a soup kettle or Dutch oven. Bring to a boil. Remove from heat, cover and let stand for ½ hour. Add vegetables, ham, garlic, parsley, thyme, bay leaf and pepper. Return to heat and simmer for 1½ hours, until lentils are tender. Garnish with parsley, eggs or sour cream.

Zucchini Soup

Makes 6 servings.

3 slices bacon, cooked and crumbled, reserve 1 tablespoon drippings
½ cup chopped onion
1 clove garlic, minced
3 cups sliced zucchini
1½ cups water
⅔ cup condensed consommé
2 tablespoons chopped parsley
¾ teaspoon chopped fresh basil or ½ teaspoon dried
Salt, optional
Freshly ground black pepper
Grated Parmesan cheese

Heat bacon drippings in a large saucepan. Sauté the onion and garlic until onion is tender. Add the zucchini, water, consommé and spices. Bring to a boil. Reduce heat, cover and simmer 15 to 20 minutes, until zucchini is tender. Puree in a blender or food processor. Return to pan and heat through. Garnish with bacon and Parmesan cheese.

Grilled Tuna Sandwiches

Makes 8 servings.

8 slices whole wheat bread
2 tablespoons softened margarine
1 clove garlic, minced
1 15-ounce can tuna, drained and flaked
8 thin slices mild Cheddar or mozzarella cheese
¼ cup tomato sauce
1 teaspoon chili powder

Toast 1 side of bread under broiler. Combine margarine and garlic and mix well. Spread margarine on untoasted sides of bread. Divide tuna among the bread. Place cheese on top. Combine tomato sauce and chili powder and mix well. Divide sauce among the sandwiches. Broil until thoroughly heated and cheese is melted.

Cheese Sandwich Soufflé

Makes 6 servings.

12 slices bread
¼ pound or more Colby or sharp Cheddar cheese, shredded
4 eggs
1 quart milk
Salt, optional
Freshly ground black pepper
¼ teaspoon sage
⅛ teaspoon paprika
1 sprig parsley, minced

Lightly grease an 8 x 12-inch baking dish. Place half the bread slices in baking dish in a single layer. Sprinkle cheese evenly on top. Place remaining bread slices on top. Beat together the eggs, milk and seasonings. Pour over bread. Refrigerate for at least 4 hours. Preheat oven to 350°. Bake 40 to 45 minutes, or until a knife inserted in the center comes out clean.

Avocado and Egg Sandwich

Makes 2 sandwiches.

4 thin slices whole wheat bread, buttered
1 ripe avocado
2 hard-boiled eggs, chilled
2 tablespoons mayonnaise
Lettuce leaves

Place avocado and egg in a small bowl and mash with a fork until thoroughly blended. Stir in mayonnaise. Spread mixture on half of the bread. Top with lettuce and remaining bread.

Cucumber-Sprout Sandwiches

Makes 2 sandwiches.

4 slices whole wheat bread
Mayonnaise
½ cucumber, sliced
⅓ cup alfalfa sprouts
Seasoning salt, optional

Spread 2 of the bread slices lightly with mayonnaise. Divide the sliced cucumber between the bread. Sprinkle each with alfalfa sprouts. Sprinkle on seasoning salt. Top with remaining bread.

Toasted Turkey Sandwiches

Makes 3 sandwiches.

½ cup minced turkey
2 teaspoons sweet pickle relish
2 tablespoons chopped celery
2 tablespoons mayonnaise
6 slices whole wheat bread
2 eggs, lightly beaten
¼ cup plus 2 tablespoons milk
½ teaspoon sugar

Combine turkey, relish, celery and mayonnaise; mix well. Spread mixture on half of the bread slices; top with remaining bread. Beat eggs, milk and sugar together. Dip sandwiches into egg mixture. Fry on a hot, buttered griddle until golden

Porcupine Meatballs

Makes 8 servings.

2 pounds ground beef
2 eggs, lightly beaten
½ cup minced onion
3 slices bread, soaked in ¼ cup milk
1 cup uncooked, long grain rice
1 cup chopped celery
1 teaspoon salt, optional
⅛ teaspoon black pepper
4 cups tomato juice

Place ground beef, eggs and onion in a large mixing bowl; mix thoroughly. Remove bread from milk and add to beef mixture; blend thoroughly. Add rice, celery, salt and pepper. Mix well. Form into 2-inch balls. Preheat oven to 350°. Place the meatballs in a casserole. Pour on tomato juice. Cover and bake 1½ to 2 hours, or until rice is tender and the meatballs are thoroughly cooked.

Favorite Tacos

Makes 10 tacos.

1 tablespoon vegetable oil
1 cup chopped onion
1 pound ground beef
½ green pepper, chopped
1 cup tomato sauce
1 teaspoon chili powder
Freshly ground black pepper, to taste
1 small head lettuce, shredded
1 cup grated sharp Cheddar cheese
1 ripe tomato, cut into small pieces
½ green pepper, chopped, optional
1 4-ounce package taco shells

Heat oil in a frying pan. Sauté onion and ground beef until meat is browned. Stir in green pepper and sauté for 1 minute. Stir in tomato sauce, chili powder and pepper to taste. Reduce heat and simmer, uncovered, for ½ hour or until sauce is thick. Preheat oven to 350°. Place lettuce, cheese, tomato and green pepper in small bowls for garnish. Place taco shells in oven for 3 minutes to crisp. Remove and fill with meat sauce and desired garnishes.

Cottage Cheese and Chives on Toast

Makes 2 sandwiches.

2 slices whole wheat or rye bread
⅔ cup small curd cottage cheese
2 to 3 tablespoons minced chives

Toast bread. Top each with equal amounts of cottage cheese. Sprinkle chives on top.

Cheese 'n' Vegetable Casserole

Makes 6 servings.

1 pound fresh spinach, chopped
1 cup chopped iceberg lettuce
1 cup chopped green onion
½ cup chopped fresh parsley
1 cup diced Monterey Jack cheese
4 eggs, lightly beaten
2 tablespoons butter, melted
Unflavored yogurt

Preheat oven to 325°. Combine the first 5 ingredients; mix well. Add eggs and mix well. Coat casserole or baking dish with melted butter. Spoon in vegetable mixture. Bake for 1 hour, until top is brown and crisp. Serve hot, topped with a dollop of yogurt.

Sloppy Joes

Makes 12 sandwiches.

1 tablespoon vegetable oil
1 cup chopped onion
1 pound ground beef
¼ cup chopped celery
¼ cup chopped green pepper
1 cup tomato sauce
⅓ cup catsup
¼ teaspoon Worcestershire sauce
¼ teaspoon chili powder

Heat oil over medium heat. Add onion and sauté until slightly softened. Add ground beef, celery and green pepper. Cook, stirring often until meat is browned. Add tomato sauce, catsup, Worcestershire sauce and chili powder; mix well. Cover and reduce heat. Simmer for about 30 minutes. Serve on hamburger buns or rolls.

Toasted Turkey Sandwiches, this page
Stuffed Mushrooms, 65
Orange Drink, 64

Turkey Tetrazzini

Makes 6 servings.

- 8 ounces spaghetti
- ¼ cup margarine
- ¼ cup minced onion
- ¼ cup whole wheat flour
- 1 cup turkey broth
- 1 cup milk
- ¼ teaspoon black pepper
- ¼ teaspoon nutmeg
- ¼ teaspoon sage
- ½ cup shredded, sharp Cheddar cheese
- ¼ pound mushrooms, sliced
- 2 cups cooked cubed turkey
- ¼ cup grated Parmesan cheese

Preheat oven to 350°. Cook spaghetti according to package directions; drain. Melt margarine in a heavy saucepan. Add onion and sauté until tender. Stir in flour. Combine broth and milk. Slowly add liquid, stirring constantly. Add seasonings, cheese and mushrooms. Simmer stirring constantly until sauce is thick and smooth. Place one-third of the spaghetti in a buttered, 2-quart casserole. Cover with one-half of the turkey, then one-third of the sauce. Repeat, ending with sauce. Sprinkle with grated cheese. Bake uncovered 30 minutes or until bubbly.

Tuna-Broccoli Casserole

Makes 8 servings.

- 1 20-ounce package frozen, chopped broccoli
- 6 tablespoons margarine
- ½ cup unbleached flour
- 3½ cups milk
- 1 teaspoon salt, optional
- ¼ teaspoon black pepper
- ½ cup grated Parmesan cheese
- ¼ teaspoon dillseed
- 2 tablespoons lemon juice
- 1 9¼-ounce can tuna, drained and flaked
- 1 recipe Dropped Baking Powder Biscuits (Recipe on page 6)

Steam broccoli until tender. Preheat oven to 375°. Melt margarine in a small, heavy-bottomed saucepan. Blend in flour and cook, stirring constantly, until golden. Slowly stir in milk; cook, stirring constantly, until thickened. Add salt, pepper, cheese, dillseed and lemon juice. Add broccoli and tuna; stir gently. Pour into a 2-quart casserole. Bake 15 minutes. Arrange biscuits on top and bake 15 minutes or until biscuits are golden and casserole is bubbly.

Squash Casserole

Makes 6 servings.

- ⅓ cup chopped onion
- 4 cups sliced yellow summer squash
- 2 cups dried bread crumbs
- ⅛ teaspoon crushed thyme
- ⅛ teaspoon crushed sage
- ¼ teaspoon crushed rosemary
- ½ teaspoon minced parsley Freshly ground black pepper
- ⅓ cup margarine, melted
- 2 tablespoons minced onion
- 1 10½-ounce can cream of chicken soup
- ¾ cup sour cream
- 1 cup shredded carrots

Steam the ⅓ cup onion and squash for 5 minutes or until squash is tender; drain and set aside. Combine bread crumbs, herbs, pepper, margarine and the 2 tablespoons onion. Preheat oven to 350°.

Spread half of the crumb mixture in the bottom of a well-greased 12 x 7-inch baking dish. Combine onion, squash, soup, sour cream and carrots. Spoon on top of crumbs. Sprinkle the remaining crumbs on top. Bake uncovered, for 30 minutes or until heated through.

Best Noodle-Cheese Casserole

Makes 6 to 8 servings.

- ½ pound egg noodles, cooked and drained
- 1 tablespoon margarine
- ½ cup minced onion
- 1 pound ground beef
- 1 cup Herbed Tomato Sauce, (Recipe on page 49)
- 1 tablespoon Worcestershire sauce, optional
- 1 cup creamed cottage cheese
- 1 cup sour cream or yogurt
- 1 3-ounce package cream cheese, room temperature
- 1 tablespoon chopped green onion or chives
- 1 tablespoon chopped green pepper

Melt margarine in a frying pan; sauté onion until tender. Add ground beef and brown. Add Herbed Tomato Sauce and Worcestershire sauce. Combine cottage cheese, sour cream, cream cheese, green onion and green pepper, stirring to blend. Arrange half of the noodles in a greased 2½-quart casserole. Spread cheese mixture on top. Layer remaining noodles. Spread meat mixture on top. Refrigerate covered at least 4 hours. Preheat oven to 350°. Bring casserole to room temperature. Bake for 1 hour or until heated through and bubbly.

Mixed Vegetable Quiche

Makes 6 servings.

2 tablespoons margarine or butter
3 cups sliced mushrooms
1 10-inch unbaked pastry shell
1 cup chopped onion
1 cup shredded zucchini
1 cup shredded carrots
1 clove garlic, minced
4 eggs, lightly beaten
1 cup milk
½ cup sour cream
1½ cups shredded Swiss cheese
¾ teaspoon salt, optional
⅛ teaspoon nutmeg

Preheat oven to 350°. Heat margarine in a frying pan; sauté mushrooms until softened. Remove mushrooms with a slotted spoon and place in crust. Add onion; sauté for 1 minute. Add zucchini, carrots and garlic; sauté until tender. Spoon vegetables over mushrooms. In a separate bowl, combine eggs, milk, sour cream, cheese, salt and nutmeg. Pour over vegetables. Bake 40 to 45 minutes or until knife inserted in center comes out clean. Let stand 10 minutes before serving.

Crepes

Makes 16 to 18 crepes.

3 eggs
1¼ cups unbleached flour
1¼ cups milk
¼ teaspoon salt
1 tablespoon vegetable oil
   Butter or margarine

Combine eggs, flour, milk, salt and vegetable oil; mix until smooth. Set aside 1 to 2 hours. Lightly grease an 8-inch crepe pan. Stir batter and pour about 2 table-spoons into pan. Lift and tilt pan so batter covers bottom of pan in a thin layer. Cook 45 to 60 seconds or until crepe is golden on bottom. Loosen edges with a spatula. Turn pan upside down over plate and let crepe fall out. Repeat with remaining batter, greasing pan as needed. Place a scant ¼ cup of Chicken Filling on center of crepe and roll up. Place crepe seam-side down in a lightly-greased 9 x 13 x 2-inch baking pan. Pour remaining broth over. Bake uncovered in a 350° oven about 15 minutes or until hot.

Chicken Filling

¼ cup butter or margarine
¼ cup chopped onion
¼ cup sliced mushrooms
3 tablespoons flour
2 cups chicken broth
½ teaspoon paprika
1½ cups chopped, cooked chicken

Melt butter in a saucepan. Add onion and mushrooms; sauté until onion is tender. Stir in flour. Gradually add chicken broth, stirring constantly. Simmer, stirring occasionally until thickened. Stir in paprika and cooked chicken.

No-Crust Ham Quiche

Makes 6 servings.

4 eggs, lightly beaten
1 cup unflavored yogurt
½ cup skim milk
1 to 2 cups chopped ham
1 pound spinach, cleaned and chopped or 1 10-ounce package frozen, chopped spinach, thawed and drained
4 tablespoons grated Parmesan cheese
4 tablespoons chopped parsley
¼ teaspoon ground nutmeg
½ teaspoon salt, optional
¼ teaspoon black pepper

Preheat oven to 350°. Combine eggs, yogurt and milk; mix well. Stir in ham, spinach, half of the cheese, half of the parsley and the seasonings. Pour into a large pie plate or 5-cup casserole. Sprinkle on remaining cheese and parsley. Place pie plate or casserole in a larger pan and fill ⅔ full of boiling water. Bake for 40 to 50 minutes or until a knife inserted in center comes out clean. Remove from oven. Let stand for 10 minutes before serving.

Tuna-Broccoli Strata

Makes 4 servings.

8 slices firm bread
1 13-ounce can tuna, drained and flaked
1 10-ounce package frozen broccoli, thawed and drained
1 cup shredded Cheddar cheese
4 eggs, lightly beaten
2 cups milk
½ teaspoon salt, optional
¼ teaspoon black pepper
¼ cup shredded Colby cheese

Preheat oven to 350°. Place 4 slices bread on the bottom of a lightly greased 9-inch baking dish. Combine the tuna, broccoli and cheese; mix lightly. Spread evenly on bread. Place the remaining bread on top of the tuna mixture. Combine eggs, milk, salt and pepper; mix well. Carefully pour into pan. Sprinkle cheese on top. Bake 40 minutes or until a knife inserted in the center comes out clean.

Fresh Herb Quiche

Makes 5 to 6 servings.

- 4 eggs, lightly beaten
- 1¼ cups light cream or evaporated milk
- ⅔ cup grated Cheddar, Parmesan, or Swiss cheese
- 5 to 6 tablespoons minced herbs such as parsley, chives, tarragon, dill or chervil
- ¼ teaspoon salt, optional
- ⅛ teaspoon black pepper
- 1 10-inch unbaked pastry crust

Preheat oven to 325°. Combine eggs, cream, cheese and herbs; mix well. Add salt and pepper. Pour into pastry crust. Bake for 40 minutes or until a knife inserted in center comes out clean. Let stand 10 minutes before serving.

Quick quiche crust: unroll a package of refrigerated crescent rolls, fit into quiche pan and fill with your favorite filling.

Individual Quiches

Makes 6 servings.

- 6 small crepes (Recipe on page 21)
- 3 bacon slices, cooked until crisp and crumbled
- ½ cup cottage cheese
- 1 tablespoon milk
- 2 eggs
- ⅓ cup grated Swiss cheese
- 1 tablespoon chopped green onions or chives
- ⅛ teaspoon freshly ground black pepper

Preheat oven to 375°. Place crepes in lightly greased muffin cups. Sprinkle half of the bacon over the bottom of the crepes. Set aside remaining bacon. Combine remaining ingredients and beat with electric mixer until smooth. Divide mixture among crepes. Sprinkle reserved bacon on top. Bake 20 minutes or until knife inserted in the center comes out clean.

Noodles Alfredo

Makes 2 to 3 servings.

- 8 ounces egg noodles
- ¼ cup margarine or butter
- ½ cup light cream
- ½ cup grated Parmesan cheese
- ⅛ teaspoon black pepper
- ½ teaspoon salt, optional
- 1 to 2 tablespoons chopped parsley

Bring 6 cups water to a rapid boil. Add noodles. Return to a boil, stirring. Boil 2 minutes covered; remove from heat. Let stand 5 to 7 minutes until just tender; drain. Melt margarine in a saucepan. Add cream, cheese and seasonings. Stir in noodles and toss. Garnish with chopped parsley.

Tuna Loaf

Makes 4 to 6 servings.

- 1 9¼-ounce can tuna, drained and flaked
- 1½ to 2 cups grated, sharp Cheddar cheese
- 1 egg, lightly beaten
- 3 to 4 tablespoons milk
- 1 tablespoon melted margarine
- 2½ cups cracker crumbs

Preheat oven to 350°. Combine all ingredients, mixing well. Turn into an 8 x 4-inch greased loaf pan and pat down firmly. Bake for 45 minutes or until golden brown.

Casseroles containing cheese should be baked at low temperatures to prevent the cheese on top from toughening.

Beef and Cheese Casserole

Makes 8 servings.

- ⅔ cup sliced, fresh mushrooms
- 1 tablespoon butter
- 1 tablespoon vegetable oil
- 2 pounds lean ground beef
- 1 cup chopped onion
- 1 clove garlic, minced
- 2 cups Herbed Tomato Sauce, (Recipe on page 49)
- 1 16-ounce can tomatoes, with liquid
- ½ pound shell macaroni, cooked and drained
- 3 cups sour cream
- ½ pound provolone cheese, sliced
- ½ pound mozzarella cheese, sliced

Sauté mushrooms in butter and set aside. Heat oil in a frying pan. Add ground beef and brown. Pour off excess fat. Add onion, garlic, Herbed Tomato Sauce, tomatoes and mushrooms. Stir and simmer 20 minutes. Preheat oven to 350°. Place half of the macaroni in a very large, deep casserole. Cover with half of the meat sauce. Spread half the sour cream over sauce. Top with slices of provolone cheese. Repeat, ending with mozzarella cheese. Cover and bake 35 to 40 minutes. Remove cover and bake until lightly browned on top.

Easy Chicken Casserole, 24

Egg Foo Yung

Makes 4 servings.

- 2 tablespoons vegetable oil
- 1 cup chopped, cooked pork
- 1 pound fresh or canned bean sprouts
- 6 eggs, slightly beaten

Heat oil in a large frying pan; stir-fry pork and bean sprouts. When thoroughly heated, add eggs. As eggs set, shape into 4 wedges. When lightly browned, turn wedges over. Serve with hot rice.

Curried Turkey

Makes 6 to 8 servings.

- ½ cup butter
- 2 pounds ground turkey
- 3 cups hot water or leftover cooking stock
  Salt, optional
- ⅛ teaspoon freshly ground black pepper
- 1 teaspoon curry powder
- 6 cups cooked rice

Melt butter in a large frying pan. Brown turkey lightly in melted butter. Add remaining ingredients, except rice. Cover and simmer 30 minutes, adding water if needed. Serve over hot rice.

Easy Chicken Casserole

Makes 4 to 6 servings.

- 3 tablespoons vegetable oil
- 1 3½ pound chicken, cut into serving pieces
- ½ pound ham, chopped
- 1½ cups chopped onion
  Freshly ground black pepper
- 1 clove garlic, minced
- 1 cup long-grain brown rice
- 6 tomatoes, chopped
- 2 cups chicken broth
- 2 cups green beans

Heat oil in a Dutch oven or frying pan. Brown chicken over medium heat. Add ham, onion, pepper and garlic. Cook, stirring occasionally, over medium heat about 5 minutes, or until onion is translucent. Stir in rice, tomatoes, chicken broth and green beans. Simmer covered for 20 minutes. Add more broth or water if necessary. Simmer about 25 minutes or until rice is tender.

Reduce cooking time by one-third for pasta that will be used in a baked casserole.

Easy Beef Casserole

Makes 6 to 8 servings.

- 1 tablespoon vegetable oil
- 1 pound ground beef
- 1 small onion, minced
- 1 10¾-ounce can cream of mushroom soup
- 1 10¾-ounce can cream of chicken soup
- ½ cup milk
- ¼ cup chopped green pepper
- ½ cup chopped celery
- 1 4-ounce can mushroom pieces, drained
- ½ cup cashew nuts
- 1 8-ounce package noodles, prepared according to package directions and drained
- ½ cup bread crumbs

Heat oil in a frying pan. Add ground beef and onion and sauté until onion is tender; drain. Add remaining ingredients, except noodles and bread crumbs; mix well. Stir in noodles. Place in a greased casserole. Sprinkle bread crumbs on top. Bake at 350° for 1 hour or until thoroughly heated.

Busy-Day Casserole

Makes 4 servings.

- 1 tablespoon vegetable oil
- 1 pound ground beef
- 1 cup chopped onion
- 1 10½-ounce can cream of mushroom soup
- 1 10½-ounce can cream of chicken soup
- 1 10½-ounce can water
- 1 12-ounce can whole kernel corn, drained
- ½ cup long grain rice
  Chow mein noodles, optional

Preheat oven to 350°. Heat oil in a frying pan. Sauté ground beef and onion until onion is tender. Stir in remaining ingredients. Spoon into a well-greased 2-quart casserole. Bake 1 hour or until rice is tender and mixture is bubbly. Sprinkle chow mein noodles over top.

Layer unfilled crepes between sheets of waxed paper. Roll up the entire stack and freeze. Thaw and fill as needed.

Spanish Rice

Makes 4 to 6 servings.

- 2 slices bacon, chopped
- ½ cup chopped onion
- 1 pound ground beef
- 1 green pepper, chopped
- 2 cups tomato juice
- ¼ teaspoon black pepper
- 2 to 3 cups cooked rice
- ½ teaspoon salt, optional

Preheat oven to 350°. Sauté bacon in a frying pan. Add onion and ground beef; sauté until meat is browned. Drain fat. Add remaining ingredients. Spoon rice mixture into a buttered 1½-quart casserole and bake 30 minutes or until heated through.

Brown Rice Pilaf

Makes 4 servings.

    2 tablespoons vegetable oil
    ¼ cup chopped onion
    1 cup brown rice, rinsed and
      picked over
    2 cups chicken broth or water
    1 bay leaf
    ⅛ teaspoon thyme
    ½ teaspoon salt, optional
    ⅛ teaspoon black pepper
    ⅓ cup chopped green pepper
    ½ cup sliced mushrooms

Heat oil in a skillet and sauté onion until tender. Stir in rice and cook 1 to 2 minutes, stirring constantly, or until rice is golden. Add broth, bay leaf, thyme, salt and pepper. Cover; reduce heat and simmer 45 minutes. Stir in green pepper and mushrooms. Cook about 5 minutes, or until rice and green pepper are tender.

When food is frozen solidly, pop it out of the freezer container, wrap and label.

Midwestern Goulash

Makes 4 servings.

    8 ounces elbow macaroni
    1 pound ground beef
    ½ cup chopped onion
    1 10½-ounce can condensed
      tomato soup
    1 16-ounce can cream-style
      corn
    ¼ cup milk
      Freshly ground black pepper

Prepare macaroni according to package directions; drain. Brown ground beef and onion in a large frying pan over medium heat, stirring often. Drain excess fat. Stir in tomato soup and corn. Stir in macaroni and milk. Heat through. Add pepper and mix well.

Brunch Beef Soufflé

Makes 4 servings.

    ½ pound lean ground beef
    ¾ teaspoon salt, optional
    ⅛ teaspoon nutmeg
      Dash black pepper
    ¾ cup skim milk
    3 eggs, beaten
    2 to 3 slices whole wheat
      bread, cubed
    2 ounces Swiss cheese,
      shredded
    2 teaspoons diced pimiento

Brown ground beef in a large frying pan; pour off drippings. Sprinkle salt, nutmeg and pepper over ground beef; set aside to cool. Add milk to eggs; mix well. Fold in bread cubes, cheese, pimiento and ground beef. Place mixture in a well-greased, 8-inch casserole. Cover and refrigerate overnight. Bake in a 325° oven for 1 hour and 10 minutes. Let stand 5 minutes before cutting into serving-sized pieces.

Hash Brown Omelet

Makes 4 servings.

    4 slices bacon
    2 cups diced raw potatoes
    ¼ cup chopped onion
    ¼ cup chopped green pepper
    4 eggs
    ¼ cup milk
    ½ teaspoon salt, optional
      Freshly ground black pepper
      to taste
    1 cup shredded sharp
      Cheddar cheese

Fry bacon in a large skillet until crisp. Remove bacon, drain and crumble; set aside. Combine potatoes, onion and green pepper. Fry potatoes in the bacon grease until crisp and brown. Beat eggs with milk, salt and pepper. Pour over potatoes. Top with cheese and bacon. Cover and cook over low heat. When egg mixture is set, loosen edges. Fold over and serve immediately.

Meatballs Supreme

Makes 6 to 8 servings.

    1 tablespoon margarine
    2 tablespoons minced onion
    ¼ pound ground pork
    1 pound ground beef
    ⅔ cup cracker or bread
      crumbs
    1 teaspoon salt, optional
    ⅛ teaspoon pepper
    ⅛ teaspon thyme
    ⅛ teaspoon oregano
    ⅓ cup milk
    1 egg
    1 tablespoon margarine
    1½ cups sour cream

Melt margarine in a large frying pan. Add onion and sauté until onion is tender. Combine remaining ingredients, except margarine and sour cream; mix well. Add onions to meat mixture; mix well. Form into 1½-inch balls. Melt margarine in the same frying pan in which the onion was sautéed. Brown meatballs gently. Drain excess fat. Stir in sour cream. Cover and simmer 1 hour. Serve over hot noodles.

Dried herbs and spices are stronger than fresh. A dish that serves four will need only about one-quarter teaspoon of a dried herb or spice.

MAIN DISHES

After the baby arrives, there may be little time to cook. You'll be glad to have easily prepared recipes that supply a large part of daily nutrition requirements. Many of the recipes are easily doubled, so freeze these dishes for those occasions when time and energy are at a premium.

Pot-au-Feu

Makes 8 servings.

- 2 pounds lean chuck, rump or brisket
- 1 to 2 pounds beef soup bones
- 10 cups beef stock or canned beef bouillon
- 1 large onion, studded with 4 cloves
- 3 cloves garlic
- 3 whole peppercorns
- 5 sprigs parsley
- 1 bay leaf
- ½ teaspoon thyme
- 1 1-inch strip orange peel
- 2 carrots, quartered
- 1 turnip, quartered
- 2 celeriac roots, cleaned and trimmed, optional
- 1 cup chopped onion
- 1 parsnip, quartered
- 1 small cabbage
  Salt, optional
  Freshly ground black pepper

Place meat and soup bones into a large soup kettle or Dutch oven. Add stock. Add onion, herbs and seasonings; bring to a boil. Turn down heat; cover and simmer 2 hours. Remove bones. Strain broth and skim fat. Add vegetables except cabbage; simmer covered 1 hour. Quarter cabbage; tie with a string to keep intact. Add cabbage and simmer 15 minutes or until tender. Add salt and pepper to taste.

Note: If using a slow cooker, cook 8 hours on high. Add vegetables except cabbage during last 3 hours. Add cabbage during the last 1½ hours of cooking.

Swedish Meatballs

Makes 48 meatballs.

- ⅓ cup dry bread crumbs
- ⅓ cup milk
- 2 tablespoons minced onion
- 1 tablespoon butter
- ¾ pound ground beef
- ¼ pound ground pork
- ¾ teaspoon salt
- ⅛ teaspoon black pepper
- 1 10¾-ounce can cream of mushroom soup
- ⅓ cup milk
- ½ cup sour cream
- 2 to 3 tablespoons butter

Combine bread crumbs and milk; set aside. Sauté onion in 1 tablespoon butter until tender. Add beef, pork, salt and pepper; mix thoroughly. Shape into 48 meatballs. Melt 2 tablespoons butter in frying pan. Fry meatballs, shaking pan to keep balls round and evenly browned. Drain fat. Stir in soup and milk. Heat just to a boil; reduce heat. Cover and simmer 15 minutes. Stir in sour cream; heat through.

To reduce the acidity of canned tomatoes, add a grated carrot. The flavor improves as does the texture and nutrition.

Lazy Day Pot Roast

Makes 4 servings.

- 1 3-pound chuck roast
- 2 tablespoons vegetable oil
- 4 carrots, quartered
- 4 small onions
- 4 parsnips, quartered
- 4 medium potatoes, pared and halved

Preheat oven to 325°. Trim fat from roast. Heat oil in a Dutch oven. Brown roast on all sides. Cover and bake 1½ hours. Skim fat. Place carrots, onions, parsnips and potatoes around roast. Cover and return to oven. Bake for 1 hour or until vegetables are tender.

Broiled Marinated Chicken, 32
Fresh fruit and vegetables

MAIN DISHES

Beef in Wine Sauce

Makes 6 servings.

2½ to 3 pounds beef chuck roast
2 tablespoons vegetable oil
1 cup chopped onion
3 cloves garlic, minced
1 rib celery
4 large carrots, quartered
1 1-pound can tomatoes
4 cups beef broth
1½ to 2 cups dry white wine
¼ teaspoon black pepper
½ teaspoon salt
1 teaspoon thyme
1 teaspoon basil
2 tablespoons cornstarch
½ cup water

Trim fat from roast. Heat oil in a Dutch oven. Brown roast on all sides. Add remaining ingredients, except cornstarch and water. Cover and simmer 3 to 4 hours or until tender. Remove meat; cool. Combine stock and vegetables in a blender container; puree. Pour puree into a large saucepan and heat. Mix cornstarch with water. Pour slowly into puree, stirring constantly, until sauce thickens. Thinly slice roast and add to sauce. Serve over hot buttered noodles.

Swiss Family Steak

Makes 6 servings.

⅓ cup whole wheat flour
¼ teaspoon salt, optional
⅛ teaspoon black pepper
2 pounds lean round steak,
   1 inch thick
2 tablespoons vegetable oil
½ cup sliced onion
¼ cup chopped green pepper
1 16-ounce can tomatoes,
   with liquid
1 tablespoon lemon juice

Combine flour, salt and pepper. Sprinkle 1 side of steak with flour and pound in. Turn steak over and pound in remaining flour. Cut meat into serving pieces. Heat oil in a skillet; brown steak on both sides. Add remaining ingredients. Cover and simmer 1½ to 2 hours or until tender.

Keep onions in a tightly covered container in the freezer. Slice them while they're frozen and you'll have no more tears.

Vegetables and Round Steak Dinner

Makes 6 to 8 servings.

2 pounds round steak, about
   ½ inch thick
2 tablespoons whole wheat
   flour
½ teaspoon salt, optional
⅛ teaspoon pepper
2 tablespoons vegetable oil
2 cups sliced onion
4 potatoes, sliced thick
4 large carrots, halved
1 bay leaf
1 cup beef broth
2 cups fresh or frozen
   green beans

Trim fat from steak. Combine flour, salt and pepper. Sprinkle half the flour mixture on one side of steak. Pound flour into steak; turn meat and pound remaining flour into other side. Heat oil in a large frying pan; sauté onion until tender. Push onion to the side; add steak and brown on both sides. Add potatoes, carrots, bay leaf and beef broth. Cover and simmer for 1½ hours or until meat is tender. Add green beans; cook an additional 20 minutes or until beans are tender.

Baked Mostaccioli

Makes 4 servings.

2 tablespoons vegetable oil
1 pound lean ground beef
1 cup chopped onion
½ cup chopped green pepper
1 1-pound can tomatoes
1 6-ounce can tomato paste
½ cup water
⅛ teaspoon black pepper
½ teaspoon oregano
¼ teaspoon basil
8 ounces mostaccioli
1 cup shredded mozzarella
   cheese
⅓ cup grated Parmesan cheese

Heat vegetable oil in a large skillet. Brown ground beef, drain and set aside. Add onion and green pepper to skillet. Sauté until onion is tender. Remove excess fat. Add tomatoes, tomato paste, water and seasonings. Stir in meat; cover and simmer 15 minutes. Preheat oven to 350°. Cook mostaccioli according to package directions; drain. Place half the pasta in the bottom of a greased 2-quart casserole. Spoon on half of the meat sauce. Sprinkle on half the mozzarella and Parmesan cheeses. Repeat layers, ending with Parmesan cheese. Bake 30 minutes or until casserole is bubbly and cheeses are thoroughly melted.

Pork Steaks with Stuffing

Makes 4 servings.

4 pork tenderloin steaks
2 tablespoons vegetable oil
⅛ teaspoon freshly ground
   black pepper
½ teaspoon salt, optional
   Stuffing
4 thick slices apple

Preheat oven to 350°. Brown steaks in oil over medium heat; add pepper and salt. Place steaks in a flat, lightly-greased baking dish. Divide Stuffing among the steaks, covering each completely. Place an apple slice on top of stuffing. Cover tightly and bake 1 hour or until pork is tender and well done.

Stuffing

 2 cups dry bread crumbs
 1 cup chopped apple
 ½ cup chopped onion
 ⅓ cup chopped celery
 ½ teaspoon salt, optional
 ¼ teaspoon thyme
 ⅛ teaspoon rosemary
 ⅛ teaspoon sage
 ⅛ teaspoon freshly ground
   black pepper
 ⅓ cup chicken broth

Combine all ingredients, except chicken broth; mix well. Add broth and toss to moisten.

Oven Beef Stew

Makes 6 servings.

1½ pounds boneless beef chuck
   cut into 1-inch cubes
 2 cups canned tomatoes with
   juice
 3 carrots, quartered
 2 ribs celery, quartered
 1 onion, sliced, optional
 ½ green pepper, sliced,
   optional
 1 slice bread
 ½ teaspoon salt, optional
 ⅛ teaspoon black pepper
 4 tablespoons quick-cooking
   tapioca

Preheat oven to 250°. Combine ingredients in a 2-quart casserole. Cover tightly and bake 6 hours. Do not uncover at any time.

Barbecued Spareribs

Makes 4 to 6 servings.

 3 pounds lean pork spareribs,
   cut into serving pieces
 1 tablespoon vegetable oil
 2 cloves garlic, minced
 2 cups sliced onion
 ¼ cup wine vinegar
 ½ cup water
 2 tablespoons brown sugar
 2 tablespoons lemon juice
 ¼ cup tomato paste
 1 tablespoon Worcestershire
   sauce
 1 teaspoon dry mustard
 2 to 3 tablespoons chili
   powder
   Salt, optional
   Freshly ground black pepper

Preheat oven to 425°. Place ribs, meaty sides up, in a shallow roasting pan. Roast uncovered until browned, about 25 minutes. Heat oil in a small saucepan and sauté garlic and onion until onion is translucent. Add remaining ingredients, mixing thoroughly. Simmer 10 minutes. Brush ribs with sauce. Reduce heat to 350°; bake about 1 hour, brushing frequently with sauce.

Layered Dinner

Makes 6 to 8 servings.

 1 cup sliced carrots
 1 cup sliced potatoes
 1 cup sliced celery
 ¾ cup brown rice
   Salt and pepper to taste,
   optional
 1 cup sliced onion
 3 cups canned tomatoes with
   juice
 ½ cup raw wheat germ

Preheat oven to 350°. Layer ingredients as listed in a buttered 2-quart casserole. Season as desired. Sprinkle wheat germ on top. Cov-

er and bake for 2 hours or until vegetables and rice are tender. Remove cover 10 minutes before baking time is completed.

Meat Loaf

Makes 6 servings.

 ¼ cup milk
 1 cup dry bread crumbs or
   cracker crumbs
1½ pounds ground beef
 ½ pound ground pork
 ¼ cup minced onion
 2 eggs, beaten
 ¼ teaspoon freshly ground
   black pepper
 1 teaspoon salt, optional

Pour milk over bread crumbs and set aside. Combine beef, pork and onion, mixing well. Add remaining ingredients, mixing thoroughly. Turn mixture into an 8 x 4-inch loaf pan. Firmly pat meat down. Bake at 350° for 1½ hours.

Macaroni with Ham

Makes 4 servings.

 ¼ cup dry bread crumbs
 1 cup hot milk
 3 tablespoons butter or
   margarine
 1 tablespoon minced onion
 1 tablespoon chopped green
   pepper
 1 cup chopped, cooked ham
 2 eggs, beaten
   Salt, optional
 2 cups cooked macaroni

Preheat oven to 350°. Combine crumbs and milk and set aside. Melt butter in a small frying pan. Add onion and green pepper; sauté until golden. Add remaining ingredients, mixing well. Spoon into a lightly greased 1½-quart casserole. Bake 30 to 40 minutes or until top is browned.

Picadillo

Makes 4 servings.

- 1 tablespoon vegetable oil
- 1 cup chopped onion
- 1 pound ground beef
- 1 clove garlic, minced
- ½ green pepper, diced
- 1 teaspoon cinnamon
- ⅛ teaspoon ground cloves
- ¼ teaspoon cumin seed
- 2 teaspoons malt vinegar
- 2 large tomatoes, chopped
- ½ cup raisins
- 1 teaspoon salt, optional
- ⅛ teaspoon freshly ground black pepper
- ⅓ cup slivered almonds

Heat oil in a large frying pan. Sauté onion and ground beef until meat is browned. Drain excess fat. Add garlic, green pepper, cinnamon, cloves and cumin seed; stir and cook for 1 minute. Add vinegar, tomatoes and raisins. Simmer uncovered about 30 minutes. Add salt, pepper and almonds; heat through. Serve over spaghetti.

All Purpose Tomato-Meat Sauce

Makes 2 quarts.

- 2 tablespoons vegetable or olive oil
- 1 pound lean ground beef
- 1 cup chopped onion
- 1 30-ounce can tomatoes
- 1 6-ounce can tomato paste
- 3 large cloves garlic, minced
- ¼ cup chopped parsley
- ¼ teaspoon freshly ground black pepper
- 1 teaspoon oregano
- 1 teaspoon basil
- ½ teaspoon fennel
- ¼ cup grated Parmesan cheese
- 1 teaspoon salt

Heat oil in a large skillet. Add beef and onion; sauté until meat is brown. Add remaining ingredients and simmer uncovered about 1 hour. Use on spaghetti, fettucini, mostaccioli, pizza, lasagna, or in dishes that call for a tomato-meat sauce. Note: This sauce can be frozen successfully. Divide among 1 or 2-cup containers for later use.

No-Yeast Pizza Crust

Makes 8 servings.

- 1 cup whole wheat flour
- 1 teaspoon baking powder
- 1 teaspoon salt
- 1 teaspoon oregano
- 2 eggs
- ⅔ cup milk
- 3 cups All-Purpose Tomato-Meat Sauce, (Recipe on this page)
- ½ cup minced green onion, optional
- ½ cup sliced mushrooms, optional
- ½ cup sliced black olives, optional
- 8 ounces grated mozzarella cheese
- ¼ cup grated Parmesan cheese

Preheat oven to 425°. Combine flour, baking powder, salt and oregano. Beat in eggs and milk; mix until smooth. Lightly grease and flour a 13-inch pizza pan. Pour batter into pan (it will be runny), spreading it to edges. Spoon meat sauce over batter; sprinkle onion, mushrooms or olives over. Bake 15 to 20 minutes or until crust is firm. Sprinkle on mozzarella and Parmesan cheeses and return to oven 10 to 15 minutes.

Julia's Lasagna

Makes 6 servings.

- ½ cup chopped onion
- 1 tablespoon vegetable oil
- ¼ pound hot Italian sausage
- ¼ pound sweet Italian sausage
- ½ pound ground beef
- 1 clove garlic, crushed
- 2 teaspoons oregano
- 2 teaspoons basil
- ½ teaspoon fennel, optional
- ¼ teaspoon black pepper
- 1 16-ounce can tomatoes
- 1 15-ounce can tomato paste Salt, optional
- 9 lasagna noodles
- 2 cups ricotta or cottage cheese
- ¼ cup grated Parmesan cheese
- 1 egg, beaten
- 2 cups shredded mozzarella cheese

Preheat oven to 375°. Sauté onion in oil until tender. Add sausages and ground beef and cook until brown; drain excess fat. Add garlic, herbs, pepper, tomatoes and tomato paste. Simmer uncovered 30 minutes, stirring occasionally. Cook noodles according to package directions. Combine cottage cheese, Parmesan cheese and egg. Reserve ½ cup of the sauce. Layer ⅓ each of the noodles, sauce, mozzarella cheese and cheese-egg mixture in an ungreased 13 x 9 x 2-inch pan. Repeat 2 times. Spoon reserved sauce on top. Bake uncovered 30 minutes. Let stand 10 minutes before cutting.

Freeze unused tomato paste by the tablespoonful on waxed paper. When frozen, transfer to an airtight freezer container. Use in sauces, soups, etc.

Spaghetti Primavera

Makes 4 servings.

- 2 tablespoons margarine
- 1 cup cut-up broccoli
- 1 cup peas
- ½ cup sliced zucchini
- ½ cup sliced mushrooms
- 1 cup chopped tomatoes
- ½ pound spaghetti
- ¼ cup chopped parsley
- 5 fresh basil leaves or
  ½ teaspoon dry basil
- ¼ teaspoon oregano
- ⅔ cup grated Parmesan cheese
- ½ teaspoon salt, optional
- ⅛ teaspoon freshly ground
  black pepper

Melt margarine in a large skillet. Sauté broccoli for 2 minutes. Add peas, zucchini, mushrooms, and tomatoes; cover and simmer. Cook spaghetti according to package directions; drain. Mix spaghetti with parsley, basil, oregano, Parmesan cheese, salt and pepper. Pour broccoli sauce over and toss gently. Serve hot with additional grated Parmesan cheese.

Zucchini Fettuccine

Makes 6 servings.

- 2 tablespoons vegetable oil
- 1 cup chopped onion
- 2 cloves garlic, minced
- 3 tablespoons chopped
  parsley
- 6 small zucchini, diced
- 2 cups Herbed Tomato Sauce,
  (Recipe on page 49)
- ½ pound ground beef
- ¼ teaspoon salt, optional
- ⅛ teaspoon black pepper
- ¾ pound fettuccine

Heat oil in a large frying pan. Sauté onion, garlic and parsley until onion is tender. Stir in zucchini and cook about 5 minutes. Add Tomato Sauce; simmer 30 minutes. Brown ground beef in a frying pan; add to zucchini mixture with salt and pepper. Cook fettuccine according to package directions; drain. Pour sauce over.

Honorable Chinese Chicken

Makes 4 to 6 servings.

- ¼ cup vegetable oil
- 1½ cups broken walnuts
- 2 large chicken breasts, boned
  and thinly sliced
- ½ teaspoon salt, optional
- 2 cups chicken broth
- 1¼ cups diagonally sliced celery
- 1¼ cups sliced onion
- ¼ cup soy sauce
- 2 tablespoons dry sherry
- 1½ tablespoons cornstarch
- ½ teaspoon brown sugar
- 1 5-ounce can sliced bamboo
  shoots, drained
- 1 5-ounce can water
  chestnuts, drained and sliced

In a large frying pan or wok, heat oil and sauté walnuts until golden. Remove walnuts and set aside. Add chicken to pan; sprinkle with salt and stir-fry 2 to 3 minutes or until tender. Remove chicken. Pour off remaining oil. In same pan, pour in ¾ cup of the chicken broth; add celery and onion and cook for 5 minutes. Combine soy sauce, sherry, cornstarch, brown sugar and remaining broth; add to frying pan. Cook until sauce thickens, stirring constantly. Add chicken, bamboo shoots and water chestnuts; heat through. Stir in walnuts. Serve on hot rice or chow mein noodles.

Oven Fried Chicken

Makes 6 servings.

- 1 3½-pound chicken, cut into
  serving pieces
- ½ teaspoon salt, optional
- ¼ teaspoon freshly ground
  black pepper
- ½ cup whole wheat flour
- ½ teaspoon paprika
- ¼ cup margarine

Preheat oven to 350°. Rinse chicken pieces and pat dry. Combine salt, pepper, flour and paprika in a bag. Drop chicken pieces into bag and shake until coated. Melt margarine in a 9 x 13 x 2-inch pan. Place chicken pieces in pan, skin side down. Bake 30 minutes. Turn chicken and bake an additional 30 minutes or until golden brown.

Broiled Marinated Chicken

Makes 4 servings.

- 2½ pounds chicken breasts,
  thighs and legs
- ½ cup vegetable oil
- ¼ cup lemon juice
- 1 tablespoon soy sauce
- 1 large clove garlic, minced
- 1 teaspoon oregano
- 1 teaspoon minced parsley
- ¼ teaspoon black pepper
- ½ teaspoon salt, optional

Wash chicken and pat dry. Combine remaining ingredients in a large bowl. Add chicken pieces, turning each to coat. Refrigerate 2 to 3 hours or overnight. Place chicken in a shallow pan, skin side down. Broil 15 to 20 minutes or until lightly browned, brushing occasionally with marinade. Turn and broil about 15 minutes more or until chicken is well-done.

Continental Chicken

Makes 4 servings.

½ cup margarine or butter
½ cup dry bread crumbs
2 tablespoons grated Parmesan cheese
1 teaspoon crushed oregano
1 teaspoon crushed sweet basil
2 cloves garlic, minced
¼ teaspoon salt, optional
2 large chicken breasts, split
¼ cup minced parsley
¼ cup minced chives
¼ cup apple juice

Preheat oven to 375°. Melt butter in a frying pan. In a shallow dish, mix together crumbs, cheese, oregano, basil, garlic and salt. Dip chicken breasts into butter, then into crumb mixture, coating thoroughly. Place chicken, skin up, in a baking dish; bake 50 to 60 minutes. Mix parsley, chives and apple juice with remaining melted butter. Pour over chicken and bake 5 minutes.

Broiled Fish with Dill

Makes 4 to 6 servings.

6 tablespoons butter or margarine
½ cup slivered almonds
2 tablespoons lemon juice
¼ teaspoon salt, optional
1 tablespoon dillweed
2 pounds fillet of sole

Heat butter in a frying pan. Add almonds and sauté until lightly browned. Add lemon juice and seasonings. Heat through and keep warm. Place sole on broiler pan. Pour half of the sauce over fish. Broil 3 inches from heat for 3 to 5 minutes, until fish flakes easily. Place fish on a serving platter. Pour on remaining sauce.

Lemony Baked Fish

Makes 4 to 6 servings.

2 pounds frozen haddock fillets
1 10¾-ounce can cream of mushroom soup
½ cup milk
1 4-ounce can sliced mushrooms, drained
1 small onion, minced
2 tablespoons lemon juice
½ teaspoon paprika
¼ teaspoon oregano
¼ teaspoon pepper
1 bay leaf, crushed
1 cup bread crumbs
½ teaspoon poultry seasoning

Place frozen fillets in a shallow, buttered baking dish. Combine remaining ingredients, except bread crumbs and poultry seasonings, in a saucepan. Simmer for 10 minutes, stirring occasionally. Pour sauce over fish. Combine bread crumbs and poultry seasoning. Sprinkle over sauce. Dot with bits of butter. Bake at 375° for 45 minutes.

Chicken Ramekins

Makes 4 servings.

2 cans chunk-style chicken
½ cup minced onion
¼ cup dry bread crumbs
2 eggs, lightly beaten
¼ cup unflavored yogurt
2 tablespoons minced parsley
½ teaspoon grated orange rind
¼ teaspoon garlic salt, optional

Preheat oven to 350°. In a bowl, thoroughly combine all ingredients; mix well. Pack firmly into well-buttered individual molds or 6-ounce custard cups. Bake for 30 minutes. Loosen edges; unmold.

Baked Flounder Amandine

Makes 3 to 4 servings.

1 pound flounder fillets
¼ cup butter, melted
¼ cup lemon juice
1 teaspoon salt, optional
2 teaspoons paprika
⅛ teaspoon black pepper
⅔ cup blanched, slivered almonds

Preheat oven to 350°. Cut fillets into serving portions. Place in a well-greased baking dish. Combine butter, lemon juice, salt, paprika, and pepper; pour over fish. Sprinkle almonds on top. Bake 20 to 25 minutes, or until fish flakes easily. Just before serving, place under broiler to brown.

_____

Cook frozen fish while it is still a bit icy in the middle. Fish takes only a few minutes longer to cook and stays moist and juicy.

_____

Poached Fish

Makes 3 to 4 servings.

1 pound fresh or frozen whiting, halibut, whitefish or cod fillets
1 cup milk
1 cup water
¼ teaspoon salt, optional

If using frozen fish, thaw. Wash and pat dry fish fillets. Combine milk, water and salt in a 10-inch skillet. Bring to a boil. Add fillets and poach until fish is opaque and flakes easily.

SALADS AND VEGETABLES

Pregnant and breast-feeding women need six servings of vegetables and fruits every day. Include dark green, leafy vegetables, deep yellow or red vegetables, vegetables high in fiber, such as celery and lettuce, and citrus fruits.

Last-Minute Italian Salad

Makes 4 servings.

    6 large mushrooms, sliced
    ½ red onion, sliced and
       separated into rings
    ¼ cup Italian Dressing, below
    1 head Boston lettuce, torn
       into bite-size pieces
    ½ pound fresh spinach, torn
       into bite-size pieces

Place mushrooms and onions in a large salad bowl. Pour dressing on top; toss lightly. Add lettuce and spinach, but do not toss. Cover with plastic wrap and refrigerate at least ½ hour before serving. Toss lightly before serving.

Italian Dressing

Makes 1¼ cups.

    1 cup vegetable or olive oil,
       or a combination
    3 tablespoons red wine vinegar
    1 tablespoon lemon juice
    2 to 3 cloves garlic, minced
    ½ teaspoon white pepper
       Cayenne pepper, to taste,
       optional
    ¼ teaspoon dry mustard
    ¾ teaspoon salt, optional
       Dash hot pepper sauce

Combine all ingredients in a jar. Cover tightly and shake well. Chill before using.

Cranberry Crown Salad

Makes 8 to 10 servings.

    4 cups cranberry juice
    1 cup water
    3 3-ounce packages orange
       flavored gelatin
    ⅛ teaspoon salt, optional
    1 11-ounce can mandarin
       oranges, drained
    1 rib celery, sliced
    1 apple, diced
    ¼ cup slivered almonds

Combine half of the cranberry juice with the water in a saucepan. Heat to a simmer. Add hot liquid to gelatin, stirring constantly. When gelatin is dissolved, add salt and remaining cranberry juice. Chill until slightly thickened. Carefully fold in oranges, celery, apple and almonds. Pour into a lightly oiled 6-cup mold. Chill until set.

Fresh Vegetable Tray

Use fresh vegetables of your choice, such as green peppers, cherry tomatoes, cucumbers, cauliflower, carrots and broccoli. Line a serving platter with lettuce. Place Cheddar and Dill Dip or Herb Dip in a small bowl. Place dip in the center of the platter. Arrange fresh vegetables on platter.

Cheddar and Dill Dip

Makes 1½ cups.

    2 tablespoons butter or
       margarine
    1 tablespoon flour
    2 tablespoons granulated
       sugar
    1 cup milk
    2 egg yolks
    1 teaspoon dry mustard
   12 ounces grated Cheddar
       cheese
    1 teaspoon dillweed

Melt butter in a saucepan. Add flour, sugar and milk. Cook over low heat, stirring constantly, until slightly thickened. Stir in remaining ingredients; mix well. Store in a tightly covered container in refrigerator.

Herb Dip

Makes 2 cups.

    2 cups sour cream
    2 tablespoons chopped green
       onion
    2 tablespoons chopped
       parsley
    1 clove garlic, minced
    2 tablespoons chopped chives
       Salt to taste, optional
       Freshly ground black pepper
       to taste

Combine all ingredients and mix well. Chill well before serving.

Fresh Vegetable Tray with Cheddar and Dill Dip

Main Dish Salad

Makes 6 to 8 servings.

- 4 to 5 cups salad greens
- 1/3 cup chopped green onion
- 1 cup chopped broccoli
- 1 cup chopped cauliflower
- 1/2 cup diced celery
- 2 apples, cored, chopped and sprinkled with lemon juice
- 1/4 cup sliced radishes
- 1/2 cup diced green pepper
- 2 cups diced, cooked potatoes
- 1 cup shredded cabbage
- 2 cups shredded Cheddar cheese
- 2 hard-boiled eggs, sliced
- 1 cup raisins
- 1 cup mixed nuts
- 1 cup fresh alfalfa sprouts
  Mayonnaise, mixed with
  1 minced clove garlic
- 1 1/2 cups croutons

Layer all ingredients, in order, in a large salad bowl. Add enough mayonnaise to lightly moisten salad. Toss gently. Serve garnished with croutons.

Spinach Salad with Feta Cheese

Makes 6 servings.

- 3/4 pound spinach
- 4 tablespoons vegetable or olive oil or 2 tablespoons each
- 2 tablespoons lemon juice
- 1 clove garlic, minced
  Freshly ground black pepper
- 1/2 red onion, thinly sliced
- 1/4 cup crumbled feta cheese

Wash and dry spinach; remove stems. Combine oil, lemon juice, garlic and pepper to taste. Place spinach in a large salad bowl; arrange onion rings and cheese on top. Pour dressing over all. Toss before serving.

Romaine and Green Pepper Salad

Makes 6 to 8 servings.

- 2 large green peppers, seeded and julienned
- 1/2 head romaine, torn into bite-size pieces
- 3 ripe tomatoes, cut into eighths
- 1/2 bunch radishes, sliced
- 1 medium sweet onion, thinly sliced

Steam green peppers until tender. Set aside. Pour half the Dressing over peppers and refrigerate. Just before serving, combine romaine, tomatoes, radishes and onion in a large salad bowl. Add peppers and dressing. Toss gently; correct seasonings. Serve with remaining Dressing.

Dressing

- 1/3 cup vegetable oil
- 1/4 cup red wine vinegar
- 2 garlic cloves, minced
- 1 teaspoon minced fresh sweet basil or 1/2 teaspoon dried
- 1/2 teaspoon oregano
- 1 tablespoon chopped parsley
  Freshly ground black pepper
  Salt to taste, optional

Combine ingredients in a jar with a lid; shake well. Refrigerate until needed.

Examples of dark green, leafy vegetables are beet greens, chard, collards, dandelion greens, mustard greens, spinach and turnip greens. These are sources of iron, folacin and magnesium.

Fruit Salad

Makes 4 to 6 servings.

- 1 orange, peeled and segmented
- 1 cup seedless grapes
- 1 large apple, cut into bite-size pieces and sprinkled with lemon juice
- 1 banana, sliced and sprinkled with lemon juice
- 1/4 cup chopped walnuts, optional
- 1/2 cup strawberry or raspberry flavored yogurt
  Lettuce leaves

Combine all fruit in a bowl. Add walnuts, if desired. Stir in yogurt. Line a serving platter or individual serving plates with lettuce. Spoon salad onto lettuce.

Chicken-Fruit Salad

Makes 6 servings.

- 3 cups cooked chicken cut into bite-size pieces
- 3/4 cup orange slices
- 1 tablespoon vegetable oil
- 1 tablespoon white vinegar
- 1/2 teaspoon salt, optional
- 1 1/2 cups cooked rice
- 1 cup small green grapes, washed
- 1/2 cup diced celery
- 1 cup pineapple tidbits, drained
- 1/2 cup toasted sliced almonds
- 1/3 cup mayonnaise
  Lettuce

Combine chicken, orange slices, oil, vinegar and salt in a large salad bowl. Cover with plastic wrap and refrigerate for at least 1 hour. Before serving, add remaining ingredients, except lettuce and toss gently. Serve on beds of lettuce leaves.

Ambrosia

Makes 4 servings.

- 1 20-ounce can pineapple tidbits
- 2 oranges, peeled and segmented
- 1 teaspoon lemon juice
- 1 cup grated coconut

Place pineapple in a serving bowl. Sprinkle oranges with lemon juice and add to pineapple; stir gently. Refrigerate covered until chilled. Drain, if desired. Add coconut and stir gently.

Fruited Tuna Salad

Makes 5 to 6 servings.

- 1 9¼-ounce can tuna, drained and flaked
- ½ cup pineapple tidbits
- ½ cup seedless green grapes
- ½ cup chopped celery
- 6 ripe olives, pitted and sliced
- ½ cup chopped nuts
- ½ cup mayonnaise
  Lettuce leaves

Combine all ingredients, except lettuce; mix lightly. Chill. Spoon onto lettuce leaves either on individual plates or in a salad bowl.

New Coleslaw

Makes 6 servings.

- ¼ cup minced onion
- 2 teaspoons lemon juice
- ½ cup mayonnaise
- 2 teaspoons cumin, caraway or dillseed
- 1 teaspoon salt
- ¼ teaspoon black pepper
- 1 medium head cabbage, shredded
- ¼ cup sliced radishes

Combine all ingredients, except cabbage and radishes. Pour dressing over cabbage and toss gently. Refrigerate covered for 1 hour before serving. Garnish with sliced radishes.

Spinach Salad

Makes 4 to 6 servings.

- 6 cups bite-size pieces spinach, washed and dried
- 1 small onion, sliced
- ¼ cup diced celery
- 3 hard-boiled eggs, sliced
  Freshly ground black pepper
- ½ cup unflavored yogurt
- 1 clove garlic, minced
- 1 teaspoon minced parsley
- 1 teaspoon minced chives
- ¼ teaspoon Worcestershire sauce
- 1 tablespoon grated Parmesan cheese
- 4 teaspoons lemon juice

Combine spinach, onion, celery and eggs in a large bowl. Cover and refrigerate until ready to serve. In a separate bowl, combine remaining ingredients. Taste and correct seasonings. Chill. Drizzle dressing over spinach; toss lightly.

Carrot and Raisin Salad

Makes 6 to 8 servings.

- 3 cups grated carrots
- 1 cup seedless raisins
- 1 tablespoon honey
- 6 tablespoons mayonnaise
- ¼ cup milk
- 1 teaspoon lemon juice
- ¼ teaspoon salt, optional

Combine carrots and raisins; toss lightly. Combine remaining ingredients in a separate bowl. Pour over carrots and raisins. Stir carefully and thoroughly. Chill thoroughly before serving.

Saucy Cauliflower

Makes 4 to 6 servings.

- 1 large head cauliflower
- 1 cup chopped onion
- 1 cup unflavored yogurt
- ⅛ cup chopped coriander
- ¼ teaspoon ground cloves
- ½ teaspoon ground cardamom
- 1 tablespoon chopped gingerroot
- 2 tablespoons vegetable oil
  Sliced tomatoes

Steam cauliflower for 10 minutes; drain. Combine the next 6 ingredients; mix well. Heat oil in a frying pan. Add yogurt mixture; simmer 6 minutes. Remove from heat and cool. Gently rub yogurt sauce over cauliflower. Place in a saucepan with 1 cup steaming liquid. Cover and simmer 30 minutes or until cauliflower is tender. Baste occasionally. Garnish with tomatoes.

Spinach Soufflé

Makes 6 to 8 servings.

- 2 packages frozen spinach soufflé
- ¼ cup butter or margarine
- 2 cups sliced mushrooms
- 1 medium onion, sliced
- 1 teaspoon dried tarragon
- 1 9-inch pastry shell

Partially thaw soufflé at room temperature. Melt butter in a saucepan. Add mushrooms, onion and tarragon and sauté until mushrooms are tender. Spoon mixture into pastry shell. Carefully spoon spinach soufflé over top. Bake 1 hour at 375°, until soufflé is puffed and golden. If necessary, place a strip of foil around the edge of the pastry shell to prevent crust from scorching.

Italian Vegetables

Makes 4 servings.

- 1 tablespoon vegetable oil
- 1 cup thinly sliced onion
- 2 large cloves garlic, minced
- 1 cup thinly sliced carrots
- 1 large zucchini, sliced
- 2 large, ripe tomatoes, quartered
- 1 green pepper, julienned
- 1 tablespoon wine vinegar
- ⅛ teaspoon dry mustard
- ¼ teaspoon basil
- 1 teaspoon salt, optional
- ¼ teaspoon black pepper

Heat oil in a frying pan over medium heat. Sauté onion and garlic until golden. Add carrots; stir and cook 3 minutes. Add zucchini, tomatoes and green pepper. Simmer covered 10 minutes or until carrots are tender. Add remaining ingredients and stir to blend.

Asparagus Amandine

Makes 4 servings.

- ¼ cup milk
- 1 10¾-ounce can cream of chicken soup
- 3 hard-boiled eggs, sliced
- 1 cup grated mild Cheddar cheese
- 1 10-ounce package frozen asparagus spears
- 1 cup sliced almonds
- ½ cup bread crumbs
- 2 tablespoons butter or margarine

Cook asparagus according to package directions; drain and set aside. Combine milk and soup; mix well. Stir in eggs, cheese and asparagus. Place in a buttered casserole. Sprinkle almonds and bread crumbs on top. Dot with bits of butter. Bake at 350° for 30 to 40 minutes, until golden brown.

Cheese-Rice Filled Tomatoes

Makes 6 servings.

- 1 cup cooked rice
- 6 large, firm tomatoes
- 1 tablespoon butter
- ½ cup chopped onion
- ¼ cup chopped celery
- 2 cups shredded process Swiss cheese
- 1 4-ounce can sliced mushrooms, drained
- 1 teaspoon salt, optional
- ¼ teaspoon marjoram
- ⅛ teaspoon black pepper

Preheat oven to 350°. Prepare rice according to package directions. Rinse tomatoes; cut out and discard stem ends. Cut a ¼-inch thick slice from the top of each tomato; set aside. With a spoon, scoop out pulp from each tomato. Drain excess liquid from pulp; set pulp aside. Set tomatoes aside to drain. Heat butter in non-stick frying pan. Add onion and celery and cook over medium heat until onion is transparent. Combine rice, tomato pulp, onion, celery, cheese, mushrooms and seasonings. Mix well. Spoon mixture into tomato shells. Cover with tomato tops. Place in lightly greased baking dish. Bake for 15 minutes, or until thoroughly heated. Garnish each tomato with a parsley sprig, if desired. Serve hot.

Broccoli with Mustard Sauce

Makes 3 servings.

- 1 chicken bouillon cube
- ½ cup water
- 1 6-ounce package frozen broccoli spears
- 2 teaspoons prepared mustard
- 1 tablespoon non-fat dry milk

Heat bouillon in ½ cup water. Add broccoli and cook until tender-crisp. Remove broccoli to a serving dish. Stir mustard and dry milk into hot liquid. Pour over broccoli.

Carrot-Celery Combo

Makes 4 servings.

- 1 tablespoon butter
- 1 cup thinly sliced carrots
- 1 cup diagonally sliced celery
- ½ cup thin green pepper strips
  Salt and pepper to taste, optional
  Dash dillweed

Melt butter in a heavy saucepan. Add carrots, celery and green pepper. Cover and simmer over medium heat about 7 minutes. Season with salt and pepper. Add dillweed. Cook over low heat until vegetables are just tender, about 5 minutes.

Nectarines and Tomatoes

Makes 4 servings.

- 4 large nectarines
- 2 cups plum tomatoes
- 1 tablespoon butter
  Salt and pepper to taste, optional
- 1 tablespoon finely chopped mint or green onion

Halve, pit and cut nectarines into generous slices. Halve tomatoes or leave whole, if desired. Melt butter in a frying pan. Add nectarines and sauté over moderate heat for 1 minute. Add tomatoes and cook until hot and glazed, about 1 or 2 minutes longer. Do not overcook. Shake pan or stir gently during cooking. Season lightly with salt and pepper and sprinkle with mint or green onion.

Broccoli with Mustard Sauce
Carrot-Celery Combo
Nectarines and Tomatoes

Potato Soufflé

Makes 4 servings.

3 tablespoons butter or margarine
4 tablespoons chopped onion
2 tablespoons flour
1 cup milk
2 eggs, separated
3 cups mashed potatoes
Salt and pepper to taste, optional

Melt butter in a frying pan. Add onion and sauté until onion is transparent. Stir in flour and cook for 2 minutes, stirring constantly. Gradually stir in milk, yolks, potatoes and seasonings. Cook over low heat until thickened, stirring constantly. Beat egg whites until stiff peaks form. Fold egg whites into potato mixture. Place in a greased casserole. Bake at 350° for 25 to 30 minutes, or until top is golden.

Baked Beans

Makes 6 servings.

2 cups dry navy beans
Water
¼ cup packed dark brown sugar
1 cup molasses
1 teaspoon dry mustard
1 cup chopped onion
¼ pound bacon

Wash and sort beans. Cover with cold water and soak overnight. Bring to a boil. Reduce heat and simmer, covered for 1 hour. Preheat oven to 300°. Drain beans, reserving liquid. Combine beans, sugar, molasses, mustard and onion. Place bacon in the bottom of a 3-quart bean pot or casserole. Pour bean mixture over bacon. Add enough reserved liquid to cover. (There should be a 1-inch space at the top of the pot.) Cover and bake 6 hours, stirring occasionally, until beans are well-flavored and most of the liquid is absorbed. During baking, add additional reserved liquid. Uncover beans the last half hour of baking.

Scalloped Tomatoes

Makes 4 servings.

4 ripe tomatoes, sliced, or
1 1-pound can, and liquid
2 tablespoons minced onion
1 teaspoon minced parsley
½ teaspoon oregano
½ teaspoon salt, optional
⅛ teaspoon black pepper
1 cup soft bread cubes or cracker crumbs

Combine all ingredients, except bread cubes, in a saucepan. Bring to a boil. Reduce heat and simmer until tomatoes are soft and ingredients are blended well. Taste and correct seasonings. Divide bread cubes among serving dishes. Spoon on tomato mixture.

Hash-Brown Potatoes

Makes 4 servings.

3 cups diced, raw potatoes
½ teaspoon salt, optional
¼ teaspoon black pepper
1 tablespoon grated onion
2 tablespoons vegetable oil
1 sprig parsley, minced

Combine potaotes, spices and onion; mix lightly. Heat oil in a small, heavy skillet. Add potatoes and pack down slightly. Fry over low heat until browned on bottom. Cut mixture in half. Turn and brown the other side. Garnish with parsley.

Wax Beans with Lemon

Makes 4 to 6 servings.

3 cups wax beans
1 tablespoon butter, melted
¾ tablespoon lemon juice
Freshly ground black pepper

Steam beans 7 to 10 minutes, or until tender. Drain. Add butter and lemon juice. Toss lightly. Season to taste and serve.

Baked Zucchini

Makes 3 to 4 servings.

2 cups sliced zucchini
1 clove garlic, minced
2 slices bread, cubed
½ cup grated Monterey Jack cheese
1 egg, lightly beaten
2 tablespoons minced parsley
2 tablespoons vegetable oil

Steam zucchini until just tender. Drain. Combine all ingredients in a lightly buttered casserole. Toss lightly. Bake at 350° for 30 minutes or until bubbly.

Broccoli and Rice

Makes 4 servings.

⅓ cup margarine, melted
1 cup grated, sharp Cheddar cheese
1 egg, lightly beaten
1 cup milk
1 small onion, diced
1 cup cooked rice
1 10-ounce package frozen, chopped broccoli, cooked

Combine margarine, cheese, egg, milk and onion; mix well. Add rice and broccoli and mix well. Spoon into a buttered casserole and bake at 350° for 1 hour.

Ratatouille

Makes 4 servings.

1½ cups peeled and diced eggplant
1 clove garlic, minced
¾ cup sliced onion
2 tablespoons vegetable or olive oil
2 cups sliced zucchini
1 cup green pepper strips
2 to 3 cups chopped, ripe tomatoes or 1 16-ounce can, drained
¼ teaspoon black pepper
½ teaspoon salt, optional
1 teaspoon minced fresh sweet basil or ½ teaspoon dried
1 teaspoon minced, fresh oregano or ½ teaspoon dried

Sauté eggplant, garlic and onion in oil over medium heat. Add remaining ingredients. Simmer covered 40 minutes or until vegetables are tender. If necessary, uncover last 5 minutes to reduce liquid. Serve hot or cold.

Peas Supreme

Makes 4 to 6 servings.

2 slices bacon, fried, drained and crumbled, reserve drippings
1 rib celery, sliced
1 cup shredded spinach
1 teaspoon flour
⅓ cup chicken broth
1 16-ounce can peas, drained
½ teaspoon seasoned salt, optional
¼ cup toasted, slivered almonds

Heat bacon drippings in a frying pan. Add celery and sauté until tender. Add spinach, cover and simmer for 5 minutes. Combine flour with broth; mix well. Stir broth into spinach. Cook until thick, stirring constantly. Add bacon, peas, salt and almonds. Mix lightly and heat through.

Herbed Broccoli

Makes 6 servings.

2 pounds fresh broccoli, cut into spears
½ cup sliced ripe olives
¼ cup dry bread crumbs
⅛ teaspoon oregano
⅛ teaspoon basil
½ cup grated Parmesan cheese
¼ cup butter or margarine, melted
1 large clove garlic, minced
1 tablespoon lemon juice

Steam broccoli until tender-crisp. Preheat oven to 350°. Arrange broccoli in a lightly-greased shallow baking dish. Sprinkle olives on top. Combine bread crumbs, herbs and Parmesan cheese. Sprinkle on top of broccoli. Combine butter, garlic and lemon juice. Pour over all. Bake uncovered for 30 minutes or until heated through.

Sweet Potato and Apple Casserole

Makes 5 to 6 servings.

5 to 6 sweet potatoes
3 cups thinly-sliced apples
¼ cup packed brown sugar
6 tablespoons margarine or butter
⅓ cup apple cider
2 tablespoons maple syrup
1 tablespoon lemon juice
1 teaspoon cinnamon
½ teaspoon ginger

Boil potatoes in water to cover about 30 minutes, or until tender. Drain, peel and slice thinly. But-ter a 2-quart casserole. Combine sweet potatoes and apples in the casserole and mix gently. In a small saucepan, combine remaining ingredients and bring to a boil. Reduce heat and simmer 10 minutes. Pour over sweet potato mixture. Taste and correct seasonings. Preheat oven to 325°. Bake covered 30 minutes or until apples are tender, basting occasionally with cooking juices.

Baked Parsnips Casserole

Makes 4 servings.

1 pound parsnips, scrubbed
2 tablespoons water
1 tablespoon old-fashioned molasses
1 tablespoon lemon juice
1 teaspoon salt, optional
¼ teaspoon black pepper

Preheat oven to 350°. Thinly slice parsnips. Place in a greased, 1-quart casserole. Combine remaining ingredients; pour over parsnips. Bake covered 15 minutes or until parsnips are tender.

Sautéed Squash and Tomatoes

Makes 6 servings.

1 cup thinly sliced onion
¼ cup margarine
1 pound summer squash or zucchini, sliced ½ inch thick
¾ teaspoon salt, optional
½ teaspoon black pepper
¾ teaspoon basil
1 cup chopped tomatoes

Sauté onion in margarine over medium heat for about 3 minutes. Add remaining ingredients; mix gently. Simmer covered about 12 minutes or until squash is tender.

If you're pregnant and still working outside the home, you will be glad for easily prepared main dishes for you and your husband. If your new baby is an addition to an already growing family, use these recipes to make a special occasion for you and dad, complete with candlelight.

High Protein Salad

- 4 cups bite-size pieces spinach, chard, collards, escarole, or lettuce
- ¾ cup cottage cheese
- 2 cups alfalfa sprouts
- 2 tomatoes, quartered
- 1 Jerusalem artichoke, peeled and diced
- ½ cup diced cucumber
- ¼ cup toasted sunflower seeds
- ¼ cup soy nuts

Arrange greens on a platter. Place cottage cheese in the center and garnish with remaining ingredients. Drizzle Dressing over all.

Dressing

- 3 tablespoons vegetable oil
- 1 tablespoon lemon juice
  Salt, optional
  Freshly ground black pepper
- ⅛ teaspoon dry mustard

Combine all ingredients and mix well.

Freeze leftover vegetables in a large freezer container. When the container is full, make vegetable soup.

Main Dish Shrimp Salad

- 1 envelope unflavored gelatin
- ½ cup boiling water
- 1 cup tomato juice
- ¼ cup lemon juice
- 2 tablespoons vinegar
- ½ teaspoon salt, optional
- 2 4-ounce cans shrimp, drained
- ½ cup chopped celery
- 2 tablespoons chopped onion
- 2 tablespoons chopped green pepper
  Lettuce leaves

Dissolve gelatin in boiling water. Stir in juices, vinegar, and salt. Chill until partially set. Stir in remaining ingredients. Chill until set. Serve on lettuce leaves.

Tomato Salad

- 2 tomatoes, peeled and seeded
- ¼ cup minced onion
- ½ teaspoon lemon juice
- 1 hard-boiled egg, sliced
  Lettuce leaves
  Grated Parmesan cheese

Chop tomatoes. In a separate bowl, combine onion, lemon juice and egg; mix lightly. Add to tomatoes. Arrange lettuce on individual serving plates. Divide tomato salad between plates. Top with Parmesan cheese.

Melon Salad

- 1 small cantaloupe, halved, seeded and cubed, reserve shells
- 2 small tomatoes, sliced
- 1 green pepper, seeded and chopped
- 2 green onions, minced
- 2 tablespoons mayonnaise
- 1 tablespoon sour cream
  Pinch ground ginger

Trim the bottom of each melon shell so that it will stand firm. Combine melon, tomatoes, green pepper and onions in a small bowl; toss lightly. Combine mayonnaise, sour cream and ginger; mix thoroughly. Spoon melon and vegetables into shells. Top with dressing. Chill for 1 hour before serving.

Carrot Salad

- 1 cup shredded carrots
- 2 tablespoons minced parsley
- 1 tablespoon minced green pepper
- 3 tablespoons bottled French dressing
  Lettuce leaves

Combine carrots, parsley and green pepper. Add dressing and mix lightly. Arrange lettuce on individual serving plates. Divide salad between plates.

Molded Vegetable Salad

1 teaspoon unflavored gelatin
⅓ cup boiling water
¼ cup lemon juice
1 teaspoon vinegar
   Salt, optional
¼ cup cooked sliced carrots
¼ cup cooked peas
2 tablespoons sliced radishes
2 tablespoons chopped onion
2 tablespoons sliced celery
   Lettuce leaves

Dissolve gelatin in boiling water. Add lemon juice, vinegar, and salt. Chill until partially set. Stir in vegetables. Pour into a 2-cup mold or individual bowls. Chill until set. Unmold onto lettuce leaves. Top with mayonnaise or salad dressing, if desired.

Fruit Cocktail Mold

2 teaspoons unflavored gelatin
⅓ cup boiling water
½ teaspoon lemon juice
1 17-ounce can fruit cocktail, drained, reserving ½ cup liquid
1 banana, sliced

Dissolve gelatin in boiling water. Add lemon juice. Combine reserved liquid and gelatin. Chill until partially set. Carefully stir in fruit cocktail and banana. Pour into a 2-cup mold. Chill until set.

Eggplant Italiano

2 teaspoons margarine
1 clove garlic, minced
1 onion, chopped
1 tomato, chopped
1 cup chopped eggplant
   Salt and pepper to taste, optional

Melt margarine in a saucepan. Add garlic and sauté for 2 minutes. Add onion, tomato and eggplant. Toss and cook until onion is tender. Season as desired.

Southern-Style Beans

½ cup dry red beans, sorted and rinsed
2 cups water
1 teaspoon salt, optional
2 slices bacon
¼ cup chopped onion
¼ cup chopped celery
¼ cup chopped green pepper
1 tablespoon chopped parsley
1 teaspoon garlic powder
1 bay leaf

Place beans in a saucepan. Add water and salt. Bring to a boil. Reduce heat and simmer for 15 minutes. Remove from heat. Let stand 1 hour. Do not drain. Stir in remaining ingredients. Bring to a boil and simmer for 2 hours. Stir occasionally. Add extra water if needed. Discard bay leaf.

Cheddary Green Beans

1 tablespoon butter
1½ cups Chinese noodles
1 16-ounce can green beans, drained
½ can Cheddar cheese soup
½ cup milk
   Salt and pepper, optional

Melt butter in a baking dish or casserole. Arrange half of the Chinese noodles in baking dish. Arrange green beans on top of noodles. Combine soup and milk; blend well. Pour over beans. Salt and pepper to taste. Top with remaining noodles. Cover and bake at 375° for 20 to 25 minutes.

Broiled Tomatoes

2 small tomatoes
1 tablespoon melted margarine
2 tablespoons dry bread crumbs
2 tablespoons grated Parmesan cheese

Cut tomatoes in half. Arrange in a small baking dish, cut side up. Brush with melted margarine. Broil until tomatoes begin to soften and brown. Sprinkle on bread crumbs and grated cheese. Broil until lightly browned.

Sweet and Sour Carrots

1¼ cups sliced carrots
2 tablespoons vegetable oil
1 tablespoon vinegar
¼ cup sugar
¼ teaspoon dry mustard
¼ teaspoon Worcestershire sauce
1 8-ounce can tomato sauce
1 tablespoon diced onion

Steam carrots until tender; drain. Combine remaining ingredients in a saucepan. Heat through. Add carrots and heat through.

Rice Parisian

1 tablespoon margarine
⅓ cup uncooked rice
¼ cup sliced mushrooms
½ package onion soup mix
1¼ cups water

Melt margarine in a saucepan. Add rice and mushrooms; sauté until rice is lightly browned. Add soup mix and water. Simmer uncovered for 30 minutes or until rice is tender.

Elegant Chicken

1 tablespoon flour
  Salt and pepper, optional
¼ teaspoon dried dillweed
2 chicken thighs or 1 whole
  breast, halved
1 egg, lightly beaten
2 tablespoons vegetable oil
¾ cup chicken broth
1 green pepper, seeded and
  julienned
2 medium tomatoes, chopped
¼ cup half and half
½ cup grated Cheddar cheese

Combine flour and seasonings; mix lightly. Dip chicken in egg and then in flour; shake off excess. Heat vegetable oil in a medium saucepan. Brown chicken in oil, turning to brown all sides. Add chicken broth and bring to a boil. Reduce heat, cover and simmer for 45 minutes, or until chicken is tender. Arrange chicken in a flameproof dish. Set aside and keep hot. Add green pepper and tomatoes to saucepan. Simmer for 5 minutes, until peppers are tender. Remove vegetables with a slotted spoon. Arrange around chicken. Stir cream into liquid in saucepan. Heat through. Pour sauce over chicken. Sprinkle on grated cheese. Broil for 5 minutes or until cheese melts.

Baked Chicken and Rice

⅔ cup quick-cooking rice
1 10¾-ounce can cream of
  chicken soup
4 pieces chicken
½ envelope onion soup mix

Combine rice and soup; mix thoroughly. Pour into a small casserole. Lay chicken on top. Sprinkle soup mix over all. Cover and bake at 325° for 1½ hours or until chicken is tender.

Broiled Chicken

2 chicken breasts, split
¼ teaspoon salt
⅛ teaspoon black pepper

Wash chicken breasts and pat dry. Sprinkle with salt and pepper. Place on broiler pan, skin side down, 5 to 7 inches from the heat. Broil 15 to 20 minutes or until lightly browned. Turn and broil about 15 minutes or until no pink shows when pierced with a fork.

Refrigerate fresh chicken loosely wrapped in waxed paper. Use within three days.

To ensure tender chicken, marinate it in milk in the refrigerator before frying or baking.

Cornish Hens

2 Cornish game hens
½ teaspoon salt, optional
¼ teaspoon black pepper
6 tablespoons butter or
  margarine
¼ teaspoon lemon juice
⅛ teaspoon paprika

Season hens with salt and pepper. Truss hens. Bring skin over neck opening and fasten with a metal pick. Tie legs together with string. Bend wings and tuck under bird. Close cavity with metal picks. In a saucepan, combine 4 tablespoons of the butter with the lemon juice and paprika; heat until butter melts. Melt remaining butter in a frying pan. Brown hens on all sides. Place hens in a large roasting pan. Brush with melted seasoned butter. Roast in a preheated 450° oven for 40 minutes or until tender.

Chicken a la King

2 tablespoons margarine
1 cup sliced mushrooms
¼ cup minced green pepper
2 tablespoons flour
  Dash black pepper
1 cup chicken broth
1 cup light cream
1 cup diced cooked chicken
2 tablespoons chopped
  pimiento, optional

Melt margarine in a saucepan. Add mushrooms and green pepper and sauté until tender. Blend in flour and pepper. Cook over low heat, stirring constantly, until mixture is smooth and bubbly. Remove from heat. Slowly stir in broth and cream. Return to heat. Bring to a boil, stirring constantly. Reduce heat; add chicken and pimiento. Heat through. Serve over noodles or rice.

Easy Curried Chicken

⅓ cup whole wheat flour
⅛ teaspoon black pepper
¼ teaspoon salt, optional
½ teaspoon curry powder
2 chicken breasts, washed and
  patted dry
2 to 3 tablespoons margarine
  or butter
1 cup chicken broth

Combine flour, pepper, salt and curry powder in a bag. Add chicken breasts and shake to coat. Melt margarine in a skillet with a cover. Sauté chicken until golden on all sides. Remove chicken. Pour leftover seasoned flour into pan and mix thoroughly. Slowly add broth, stirring constantly. Return chicken to pan. Cover and simmer until chicken is tender, 45 to 55 minutes.

Chicken Veronica

- 2 whole chicken breasts, split in half
- 1¼ cups dry white wine
- ⅛ teaspoon rosemary
- 2 tablespoons butter or margarine
- 2 tablespoons whole wheat flour
- ¼ teaspoon nutmeg
- ¼ teaspoon black pepper
- 1 teaspoon salt
- 1 cup seedless green grapes

Wash chicken breasts and pat dry. Place in a large skillet. Add wine and rosemary. Simmer covered 30 minutes or until chicken is tender. Remove chicken from broth and keep warm. Melt butter in a small, heavy-bottomed saucepan; stir in flour. Cook several minutes, stirring constantly. Stir in wine broth left from chicken. Add seasonings and grapes. Heat, until sauce thickens, stirring occasionally. Pour over chicken. Serve with rice.

For added flavor and vitamin C, substitute freshly squeezed juice for part of the water in gelatin salads.

Ham and Pork Loaf

- ½ pound pork sausage
- ½ pound ground ham
- 1 egg
- ½ cup finely crushed cornflakes
- 2 tablespoons evaporated milk
- Pepper to taste

Combine all ingredients in a mixing bowl. Stir until well blended. Spoon into a small loaf pan or casserole; pack down slightly. Bake at 350° for 1 hour.

Chicken Parmigiana

- 1 whole boneless chicken breast, skinned and cut in half
- ¼ cup whole wheat flour
- 1 egg, beaten
- ⅓ cup bread crumbs mixed with 1 tablespoon Parmesan cheese
- 2 tablespoons butter
- 1 cup Herbed Tomato Sauce (Recipe on page 49)
- 2 slices mozzarella or fontina cheese
- Grated Parmesan cheese

Place each chicken breast between 2 pieces of plastic wrap. Pound lightly. Dip into flour, then egg, and finally into bread crumb mixture. Heat butter in a small skillet. Brown chicken on both sides. Preheat oven to 350°. Place chicken in a shallow baking dish. Bake about 10 minutes. Pour Tomato Sauce over chicken. Place cheese slices on top; bake until cheese is bubbly. Serve with extra Parmesan cheese, if desired.

Herbed Flank Steak

- 1½ pounds flank steak
- 1 tablespoon vegetable oil
- 1 clove garlic, minced
- 2 tablespoons minced parsley
- 1 green onion, chopped
- 1 teaspoon lemon juice
- Salt, optional
- Freshly ground black pepper

Place steak in a shallow dish. Combine oil, garlic, parsley, onion and lemon juice. Brush mixture on both sides of the steak. cover and marinate at least 3 hours at room temperature or overnight in refrig-

erator. Turn steak several times, brushing with marinade. About 10 minutes before serving, broil steak 3 inches from heat until brown, about 5 minutes. Turn steak; brush with remaining marinade and broil 5 minutes. Season with salt and pepper to taste. Slice diagonally into very thin slices.

Flaming Veal

- 2 tablespoons brandy
- 1 pound cubed veal
- 2 tablespoons butter

Heat brandy in small saucepan. Heat butter in a flameproof casserole. Quickly brown veal cubes. Ignite brandy with a match. Pour over veal.

Saltimbocca

- 2 thin veal cutlets
- 2 fresh sage leaves
- 2 fresh basil leaves
- 4 paper-thin slices prosciutto or ham
- Juice of 1 lemon
- ¼ teaspoon black pepper
- 2 tablespoons butter

Pound cutlets until very thin. Top with sage and basil leaves. Place two slices prosciutto on top of each cutlet. Sprinkle with 1 teaspoon lemon juice and ⅛ teaspoon pepper. Melt butter in a frying pan. Brown cutlets on 1 side; turn. Sprinkle ⅛ teaspoon pepper and 2 teaspoons lemon juice over both cutlets. When second side has browned, remove to heated dinner plates. Add remaining lemon juice to the pan; quickly cook lemon juice with pan juices. Pour sauce over veal.

JUST FOR TWO

Lamb Stew

¾ pound cubed lamb
1 small onion, quartered
2 carrots, sliced
2 potatoes, quartered
2 turnips, quartered
1 teaspoon salt, optional
½ teaspoon marjoram
¼ teaspoon black pepper
3 cups water
2 tablespoons flour

Place all ingredients, except water and flour in a Dutch oven or casserole. Add 2½ cups of the water. Cover and bake at 375° for 1 hour. Combine remaining ½ cup water and flour and mix well. Stir into stew. Bake 30 minutes, or until vegetables are tender.

Pepper Steak

¼ cup butter or margarine
1 pound tenderloin steak, cut into thin strips
¼ cup flour
1 green pepper, seeded and sliced
1 small onion, sliced
3 large mushrooms, sliced
1 tomato, peeled and quartered
1 cup beef broth
3 tablespoons Burgundy wine
Salt and pepper to taste, optional

Melt butter in a frying pan. Dredge steak in flour. Brown on both sides. Remove from frying pan. Add green pepper, onion, mushrooms, and tomato. Sauté for 2 minutes. Combine remaining flour with beef broth and mix well. Add broth mixture and wine to frying pan. Cover and simmer 10 minutes or until slightly thickened. Return steak to pan. Cover and simmer until meat is tender and sauce thickened.

Easy Boiled Dinner

1½ pounds chuck roast
2 tablespoons shortening
2 carrots, pared
2 small onions
2 ribs celery
2 potatoes, pared and halved
½ small head cabbage, cored
1 bay leaf
2 cups water
Salt and pepper, optional

Heat shortening in a heavy saucepan. Brown roast on both sides. Add remaining ingredients. Cover tightly and bake at 375° for 1½ hours. Place roast on serving platter. Arrange vegetables around roast.

Ground Sirloin in Wine Sauce

¾ pound ground sirloin
2 tablespoons blue or Roquefort cheese
2 tablespoons butter or margarine
½ cup dry red wine
⅓ cup finely minced green onion
2 tablespoons minced parsley
2 tablespoons chopped green pepper
1 clove garlic, minced
2 teaspoons Worcestershire sauce

Shape meat into 4 thin patties. Place 1 tablespoon blue cheese in center of 2 patties. Top with remaining 2 patties; seal edges firmly. Melt butter in a heavy frying pan; fry patties about 3 minutes on each side or until done as desired. Remove to heated plates and keep warm. Add wine and vegetables to frying pan and cook, stirring, until green pepper is just tender. Add Worcestershire sauce. Pour sauce over patties and serve.

Sunday Pot Roast

1½ pounds beef rump roast, fat trimmed
2 tablespoons flour
2 tablespoons liquid shortening
1 teaspoon salt, optional
½ teaspoon onion salt
¼ teaspoon crushed oregano
¼ teaspoon crushed thyme
¼ teaspoon sweet basil
Freshly ground black pepper
⅛ teaspoon paprika
1 16-ounce can tomatoes
½ cup water

Dust roast with flour. Heat shortening in a Dutch oven. Brown roast on all sides. Add remaining ingredients. Cover tightly and simmer for 2½ hours or until meat is tender. Turn roast occasionally. Place on a serving platter. Spoon tomato mixture on top.

Calves' Liver with Onion

2 tablespoons margarine or butter
1 cup chopped onion
1 clove garlic, minced
¼ cup cornstarch
2 ¼-inch thick slices calves' liver
Salt, optional
Freshly ground black pepper

Melt 2 tablespoons margarine or butter in a frying pan; sauté onion and garlic until onions are tender. Dust both sides of liver with cornstarch. Push onions to side; add liver. Add more butter if necessary. Fry for about 8 minutes on one side. Turn and cook approximately 8 minutes longer or until center of liver is still slightly pink. Salt and pepper to taste before removing from pan. Pour onions over liver and serve.

Ground Beef Supreme

1 slice bread
2 tablespoons milk
2 tablespoons minced onion
¾ pound lean ground chuck
1 egg
1 tablespoon grated Parmesan cheese
⅛ teaspoon black pepper
⅛ teaspoon salt, optional
¼ cup whole wheat flour
1 egg, beaten
¼ cup dry bread crumbs
2 tablespoons margarine or butter
1 cup Herbed Tomato Sauce, (Recipe on page 49)

Combine bread and milk and set aside. Combine onion, meat, egg, Parmesan cheese and seasonings. Add bread and mix well. Form into two patties. Dip patties in flour, then into beaten egg and finally into bread crumbs. Melt margarine in frying pan; fry patties over medium heat to desired doneness, about 3 minutes on each side. Pour Tomato Sauce over; heat through.

Herbed Tomato Sauce

Makes 3 cups.

3 tablespoons vegetable or olive oil
¾ cup chopped onion
3 large cloves garlic, minced
1 tablespoon minced parsley
8 to 10 very ripe tomatoes, chopped
1 teaspoon basil
1 teaspoon oregano
¼ teaspoon fennel
½ teaspoon salt, optional
¼ teaspoon black pepper

Heat oil in a frying pan. Sauté onion and garlic until onion is tender. Add parsley and tomatoes; cook briskly about 5 minutes. Lower heat; add remaining ingredients. Simmer, stirring occasionally, until sauce is thick. Serve sauce over pasta, in dishes calling for a tomato sauce, or freeze for later use.

Steak Diane

1 pound Porterhouse, T-bone, club, sirloin or tenderloin steak, about 1 inch thick
2 tablespoons butter
2 cloves garlic, minced
1 tablespoon Worcestershire sauce
2 tablespoons chopped parsley
1 tablespoon light cream or yogurt
Freshly ground black pepper

Slash fatty edges of the steak. Do not cut into meat. Pound steak. Melt butter in a frying pan; add garlic and sauté. Add steak and brown on both sides. Add Worcestershire sauce, moving steak around to absorb all the juices. Cook to desired doneness, about 3 to 4 minutes on each side. Transfer to a heated platter; sprinkle parsley on top. Stir cream and pepper into pan juices; heat. Pour sauce over steak and serve.

Stuffed Steak

2 club steaks
2 tablespoons butter or margarine
1 tablespoon chopped onion
1 tablespoon chopped celery
1 2-ounce can mushrooms, drained and finely chopped
½ cup bread crumbs

Cut a pocket in each steak. Melt butter in small frying pan. Add onion, celery and mushrooms. Sauté until onion is tender. Add bread crumbs. Sauté until butter is absorbed. Stuff pockets with crumb mixture. Secure with toothpicks. Broil until desired doneness.

Marinated Minute Steak

2 teaspoons wine vinegar
2 tablespoons vegetable oil
2 cloves garlic, minced
2 minute steaks
¼ cup whole wheat flour
⅓ cup tomato sauce
½ cup sliced onion
½ teaspoon basil

Combine vinegar, vegetable oil and garlic. Add steaks, turning to coat both sides. Marinate 15 minutes. Heat oil in a frying pan. Dredge steaks in flour; brown on both sides. Add tomato sauce, onion and basil. Simmer covered 15 minutes.

Veal Express

¾ pound boneless veal shoulder, trimmed and cut into 1-inch cubes
1 cup orange juice
½ cup beef broth
Salt, optional
Freshly ground black pepper

Combine veal, juice and broth in a frying pan with a tight-fitting cover. Simmer for 2 hours or until meat is tender. If you wish to thicken juices, remove cover the last 15 minutes. Add salt and pepper before serving. Serve over hot rice.

Easy Veal Parmesan

1 egg
½ cup dry bread crumbs
⅛ cup grated Parmesan cheese
2 veal cutlets
1 tablespoon vegetable oil
1 8-ounce can tomato sauce
2 slices mozzarella cheese
⅛ teaspoon oregano
1 teaspoon minced parsley
1 clove garlic, minced
¼ teaspoon basil
Grated Parmesan cheese

Preheat oven to 325°. Beat egg in a flat dish. Combine crumbs and Parmesan cheese on waxed paper. Dip veal in egg, then in crumb mixture. Heat oil in a frying pan. Brown cutlets on each side. Pour half of the tomato sauce into a small, flat baking dish. Place veal on top. Lay mozzarella cheese on top of veal. Combine oregano, parsley, garlic and basil with remaining tomato sauce. Pour tomato sauce over all. Sprinkle additional Parmesan cheese on top; bake 45 minutes or until sauce is bubbly.

Veal Piccata

2 veal cutlets
2 tablespoons fresh lemon juice
2 tablespoons margarine
Freshly ground black pepper
Salt, optional
1 tablespoon lemon juice
2 tablespoons beef broth
¼ cup dry white wine
3 to 4 thin lemon slices
1 tablespoon minced parsley

Pound veal until very thin. Rub veal with 2 tablespoons lemon juice; set aside 5 minutes. Melt margarine in a frying pan. Drain lemon juice from veal and brown on both sides. Season to taste with pepper and salt. Add 1 tablespoon lemon juice, broth, wine and lemon slices. Reduce heat and simmer covered 1 or 2 minutes. Serve on a bed of rice, buttered noodles or Noodles Alfredo (Recipe on page 22). Garnish with parsley.

Osso Buco

1 large veal shank, sawed into 2½-inch pieces
¼ cup whole wheat flour
2 tablespoons butter
½ cup dry white wine
1 16-ounce can tomatoes
2 cloves garlic, minced
1 small strip lemon peel
¼ cup chopped parsley
½ teaspoon basil
½ teaspoon salt, optional
⅛ teaspoon black pepper

Roll veal in flour. Melt butter in a large frying pan. Add veal and brown evenly. Add wine. Simmer covered for about 15 minutes. Add tomatoes; simmer covered 2 hours. Combine garlic, lemon peel, parsley, basil, salt and pepper. Sprinkle over meat, and turn to distribute flavors. Remove meat. Cook sauce left in pan until it thickens slightly. Pour over meat. Serve with Risotto Milanese.

Risotto Milanese

2 tablespoons butter
⅓ cup chopped onion
1 cup rice
2 cups beef broth
¼ cup grated Parmesan cheese

Melt butter in a frying pan; sauté onion until tender. Add rice and stir for several minutes until it browns. Slowly add beef broth, stirring constantly. Cover and cook over low heat 20 minutes or until rice is tender. Remove from heat and stir in cheese.

Shrimp-Stuffed Cod

1 tablespoon butter
⅓ cup chopped onion
¼ cup chopped celery
¼ cup chopped mushrooms
½ cup shrimp
2 tablespoons fresh bread crumbs
2 tablespoons minced parsley
⅛ teaspoon thyme
½ teaspoon salt, optional
⅛ teaspoon black pepper
1 pound fresh or frozen cod fillets, thawed
¼ cup butter

Preheat oven to 400°. Melt butter in a frying pan; sauté onion and celery until tender. Add mushrooms and shrimp; cook until the shrimp just turns pink and the mushroom juice has evaporated. Stir in bread crumbs, parsley and seasonings. Divide the mixture among fillets. Fold over and secure edges with skewers or string. Place fillets in a buttered baking dish; dot with butter. Bake uncovered until fish flakes easily with a fork, about 35 minutes.

Do not hesitate to trim off all possible fat before cooking meat. It is not the lack of fat that makes meat dry, it's overcooking.

JUST FOR TWO

Shrimp with Dill

2 tablespoons butter or margarine
  Salt and white pepper to taste, optional
¼ teaspoon minced onion
¼ cup dry sherry
1 teaspoon lemon juice
½ teaspoon dillweed
2 egg yolks
½ cup half and half
½ pound cooked shrimp

Melt butter in a frying pan. Add salt, pepper and onion. Sauté until onion is tender. Add sherry, lemon juice and dillweed. Cook over low heat for 2 minutes. Combine egg yolks and cream in mixing bowl. Beat until thick. Slowly pour egg mixture into frying pan. Cook over low heat until slightly thickened. Fold in shrimp. Cook 5 minutes. Spoon into timbale cups or use as crepe filling.

Sherried Sole

¼ cup butter or margarine
1 small onion, chopped
¾ cup milk
2 tablespoons flour
1 pound sole, skinned and cut into small pieces
½ teaspoon paprika
¼ cup dry sherry
2 tablespoons grated Parmesan cheese
  Salt and pepper to taste, optional
¼ cup bread crumbs

Melt butter in a frying pan. Sauté onion until tender. Combine ¼ cup of the milk with flour and blend thoroughly. Add remaining milk to frying pan. Stir in flour mixture and cook until smooth, stirring constantly. Add sole, paprika, sherry, cheese, salt and pepper. Cook over low heat until slightly thickened, stirring constantly. Pour into a lightly buttered casserole. Sprinkle bread crumbs on top. Broil until top is golden.

Broiled Halibut

2 halibut steaks
1 tablespoon lemon juice
¼ pound butter
1 clove garlic, minced
  Salt and white pepper, to taste
1 teaspoon snipped parsley
¼ teaspoon paprika

Place fish on a greased broiling pan. Sprinkle with lemon juice. Melt butter in a small saucepan. Add garlic, salt and white pepper. Sauté for 5 minutes. Brush garlic butter over halibut. Broil 10 minutes, basting occasionally with garlic butter. Turn and repeat for second side. Sprinkle with parsley and paprika before serving.

Curried Shrimp

2 tablespoons butter or margarine
1 cup chopped onion
2 cloves garlic, minced
1 green pepper, chopped
1 16-ounce can tomatoes and juice
2 tablespoons minced parsley
2 teaspoons curry powder
½ teaspoon cumin
½ pound frozen cooked shrimp

Melt butter in a frying pan. Sauté onion until golden. Add remaining ingredients, except shrimp; simmer covered until vegetables are tender. Add shrimp and heat through. Serve over rice.

Scallops Provencale

2 tablespoons olive or vegetable oil
1 large clove garlic, minced
1 green onion or shallot, minced
½ pound sea or bay scallops, rinsed thoroughly, drained, patted dry, and quartered, if large
1 teaspoon lemon juice
1 medium tomato, chopped
  Salt, optional
  Freshly ground black pepper
  Fresh parsley, minced

Heat oil in a large skillet; sauté garlic and green onion until tender. Add scallops and sauté until opaque, about 5 minutes. Stir in remaining ingredients, except salt, pepper and parsley. When heated, add salt and pepper as desired. Garnish with minced parsley.

For the whitest rice, add a few drops of lemon juice to the cooking water.

Herbed Baked Fish

⅔ cup cracker or fine bread crumbs
¼ cup grated Parmesan cheese
½ teaspoon basil
½ teaspoon oregano
1 garlic clove, minced
1 pound sole, perch, or haddock fillets
¼ cup melted butter or margarine

Preheat oven to 350°. Combine crumbs, cheese, basil, oregano and garlic. Rinse fish and pat dry. Dip fillets into melted butter. Coat both sides of fish with crumb mixture. Arrange in a greased casserole. Bake 25 to 30 minutes or until fish flakes easily with a fork.

Raisin Honey Drops

¾ cup sugar
¾ cup butter or margarine
¾ cup honey
1 egg
2 cups flour
1 teaspoon cinnamon
½ teaspoon baking soda
½ teaspoon salt
2 cups rolled oats
1 cup raisins

Cream sugar and butter. Add honey and egg; beat thoroughly. Sift together flour, cinnamon, baking soda and salt. Stir into honey mixture. Stir in rolled oats and raisins. Drop by teaspoonsful onto a greased baking sheet. Bake at 375° for 12 to 14 minutes or until lightly browned.

Dress up a fruit salad by spooning on unflavored yogurt or yogurt with added fruit.

Lemon Cloud

1 teaspoon unflavored gelatin
¼ cup boiling water
1 egg, separated
3 tablespoons granulated sugar
⅓ cup milk
½ teaspoon vanilla
2 tablespoons grated lemon rind
2 tablespoons lemon juice

Dissolve gelatin in boiling water; set aside. Combine egg yolk, sugar and milk in a saucepan. Cook until mixture thickens; stir constantly. Remove from heat. Add gelatin and remaining ingredients; mix well. Cool slightly. Beat egg white until stiff; fold into lemon mixture. Pour into two dessert dishes. Refrigerate until firm.

Pecan Meltaway

¾ cup granulated sugar
⅓ cup water
8 ounces pecans, chopped fine
½ teaspoon vanilla
8 phyllo leaves
1 cup butter or margarine, melted

Combine sugar and water in a small saucepan. Cook over medium heat until sugar is dissolved and mixture is slightly thickened, stirring constantly. Stir in pecans. Cook until thick, stirring constantly. Remove from heat. Stir in vanilla. Place 1 phyllo leaf on a damp cloth. Brush with butter. Place another phyllo leaf on top and brush with butter. Repeat until all phyllo leaves are used. Spoon pecan mixture over phyllo to within 1 inch of edge. Fold in ends. Roll up jelly-roll fashion. Place on a greased baking sheet. Curve into a horseshoe. Score into serving pieces with a sharp knife. Bake at 375° for 30 minutes.

When cutting back on sugar, add extra vanilla to a dessert recipe. The dessert will seem sweeter than it actually is.

Oatmeal Squares

Makes 18.

½ cup flour
½ cup oatmeal
⅓ cup packed brown sugar
½ cup butter, melted

Combine all ingredients in a mixing bowl; mix well. Press into a 9-inch square baking pan. Bake at 325° for 30 minutes or until golden. Cool and cut into squares.

Fresh Fruit Compote

1 pear, seeded and cut into eighths
1 peach, pitted and quartered
1 nectarine, pitted and quartered
2 apricots, pitted and halved
2 plums, pitted and halved
⅓ cup water

Combine fruits and water in a saucepan. Bring to a boil over medium heat. Reduce heat and simmer for 4 minutes. Serve hot or cold, topped with whipped cream, if desired.

Baked Apples

2 large cooking apples
¼ cup packed brown sugar
2 teaspoons butter or margarine
½ cup water

Core apples but leave whole. Pack cavity with brown sugar. Place in a baking dish. Top each apple with 1 teaspoon butter. Add water to dish. Cover tightly. Bake at 400° for 30 minutes, until tender.

Jiffy Bars

Makes 18.

1 cup flour
1 cup sugar
1 cup nuts
1 cup raisins
2 eggs
2 tablespoons milk
2 teaspoons baking powder
2 teaspoons liquid shortening

Combine all ingredients in a 9-inch square baking pan. Stir with a fork until completely mixed. Bake at 350° for 35 minutes or until golden. Cut into 2-inch bars.

DESSERTS

Fresh fruit, cheese and crackers, or even yogurt can complete a meal and keep even the greatest dessert fiend perfectly satisfied. But, if it's homemade desserts you crave, add variety by making them yourself from vegetables, fruits, seeds, nuts or wheat germ and create a nutritious and delicious ending to any meal.

Texas Apple Pie

Makes 1 9-inch pie.

- **2 single pie crusts**
- **4 pounds cooking apples**
- **2 teaspoons lemon juice**
- **¼ cup whole wheat flour**
- **¼ teaspoon nutmeg**
- **¾ teaspoon cinnamon**
- **¼ teaspoon salt**
- **⅔ cup packed brown sugar**
- **1 tablespoon butter**

Preheat oven to 400°. Line a 9-inch pie plate with 1 crust. Core and slice apples. Sprinkle with lemon juice to keep them from turning brown. Mix together flour, nutmeg, cinnamon, salt and sugar. Stir into apples. Place apples in pie shell. Dot with bits of butter. Place top crust over apples. Seal and flute edges. Prick top crust with a fork. Bake 40 to 45 minutes or until crust is browned and apples are tender.

For a delicious, low-calorie whipped topping substitute, beat a sliced, very ripe banana and an egg white until stiff and banana is completely dissolved.

Old-Fashioned Pumpkin Pie

Makes 1 10-inch pie

- **2 cups canned pumpkin**
- **⅔ cup packed brown sugar**
- **½ teaspoon salt**
- **1 teaspoon cinnamon**
- **¾ teaspoon ginger**
- **¾ teaspoon nutmeg**
- **¼ teaspoon ground cloves**
- **3 eggs, beaten**
- **1 13-ounce can evaporated milk**
- **1 10-inch, unbaked pie crust**

Preheat oven to 400°. Combine pumpkin, sugar, salt and spices. Gradually stir in eggs and milk; mix well. Pour into pastry shell. Bake 50 minutes or until a knife inserted in the center comes out clean.

Carob Cookies

Makes 18 cookies.

- **½ cup butter or margarine**
- **⅓ cup firmly packed brown sugar**
- **1 egg**
- **1 cup unbleached flour**
- **1 teaspoon baking powder**
- **2 tablespoons carob powder**
- **¼ teaspoon vanilla**

Cream butter and sugar together until light and fluffy. Beat in egg. Add remaining ingredients and mix well. Preheat oven to 350°. With floured hands, roll mixture into 1-inch balls. Place on greased baking sheets. Flatten the balls with a fork dipped in cold water. Bake 10 minutes or until golden.

Fresh Fruit Pie

Makes 4 to 6 servings.

- **1½ cups crushed graham crackers**
- **¼ cup melted margarine**
- **2 teaspoons sugar**
- **1 cup grapes**
- **1 cup blueberries**
- **1 cup strawberries, halved**
- **2 fresh peaches, sliced**

Combine graham cracker crumbs, margarine and sugar in a small bowl. Mix until thoroughly blended. Press crumb mixture into a 9-inch pie plate. Bake at 350° for 10 minutes, or until lightly browned. Arrange fruit over crust. Drizzle on Glaze.

Glaze

- **3 tablespoons currant jelly**
- **2 tablespoons water**

Combine jelly and water in a small saucepan. Cook over low heat for 3 minutes.

Cottage Cheesecake

Makes 12 servings.

     2 cups finely crushed graham
        cracker crumbs
    ¼ cup packed brown sugar
     1 teaspoon cinnamon
    ½ cup margarine, melted
     6 eggs
     1 cup packed brown sugar
    ⅛ teaspoon salt
     2 teaspoons lemon juice
     1 teaspoon vanilla
     2 teaspoons grated lemon rind
  1¼ cups milk or yogurt
     2 pounds cottage cheese
     5 tablespoons flour

Preheat oven to 350°. Combine graham cracker crumbs, ¼ cup brown sugar, cinnamon and margarine. Mix well. Press into bottom of an 8 x 13-inch baking pan. Combine eggs and 1 cup brown sugar; mix thoroughly. Add remaining ingredients, except cottage cheese and flour; mix well. Place cottage cheese in blender or bowl of a food processor; mix until smooth. Mix in flour. Add cottage cheese to egg mixture; mix well. Pour into prepared crust. Bake for 1 hour or until center is firm. Turn off heat. Open the oven door and leave cheesecake in oven until cool.

Carrot Cake

Makes 1 9-inch cake.

  1¼ cups whole wheat flour
     2 teaspoons baking powder
     1 teaspoon cinnamon
    ¼ teaspoon allspice
    ¼ teaspoon ground cloves
     1 teaspoon grated orange rind
    ⅛ teaspoon salt
    ¾ cup vegetable oil
    ¾ cup packed brown sugar
     2 eggs
     1 cup finely grated carrots

Preheat oven to 350°. Combine dry ingredients in a large bowl; mix well. Combine oil and sugar in a mixing bowl; blend thoroughly. Add eggs one at a time, beating well after each addition. Gradually add dry ingredients, mixing well. Stir in grated carrots; mix well. Pour into a greased 9-inch square cake pan. Bake 35 minutes or until top springs back when pressed lightly and edges pull away from the side of the pan. Cool cake in pan for 15 minutes. Turn out onto cake plate and frost with following frosting.

Cream Cheese Frosting

     1 3-ounce package cream
        cheese, softened
     4 tablespoons margarine
     2 cups confectioners' sugar
     1 teaspoon vanilla

Cream together cream cheese and margarine. Gradually beat in sugar. Add vanilla and beat until smooth and creamy.

Gingerbread

Makes 16 pieces.

    ½ cup milk
  1½ teaspoons vinegar
    ½ cup butter or margarine,
        at room temperature
    ½ cup granulated sugar
     1 egg
    ½ cup molasses
  1¼ cups unbleached flour
    ½ teaspoon ginger
    ½ teaspoon cinnamon
    ½ teaspoon salt
     1 teaspoon baking soda

Preheat oven to 350°. Combine milk and vinegar; set aside to clabber. Cream butter with sugar until light and fluffy. Add egg and beat until fluffy. Add milk and beat until fluffy. Add milk and mix well. Stir in molasses. Sift together dry ingredients. Gradually add to liquid mixture, mixing well. Spoon mixture into a lightly-greased 8-inch square baking pan. Bake 20 to 25 minutes or until the gingerbread springs back.

Easy Cheesecake

Makes 16 servings.

     1 cup finely crushed graham
        cracker crumbs
    ¼ cup toasted wheat germ
     1 13-ounce can evaporated
        milk, chilled
     3 tablespoons melted butter
     1 8-ounce package cream
        cheese, at room temperature
    ¾ cup granulated sugar
     1 teaspoon vanilla
     1 tablespoon lemon juice
     1 3-ounce package lemon
        gelatin
    ½ cup boiling water

Place a medium-sized mixing bowl and beaters in freezer to chill. Lightly grease a 9 x 13-inch cake pan. Combine graham cracker crumbs, toasted wheat germ and butter; mix well. Sprinkle over the bottom of the cake pan, reserving ¼ cup of the crumbs for the top. Press crumbs lightly into pan. Whip chilled milk until thickened; place in freezer. Place cream cheese, sugar, vanilla and lemon juice in blender container or small mixing bowl. Place lemon gelatin in a small bowl. Pour in boiling water and mix until gelatin is dissolved. Pour gelatin mixture into blender container; blend on high until thoroughly mixed. Gently combine whipped milk with lemon mixture. Pour into pan. Sprinkle reserved crumbs on top. Cover with plastic wrap and chill 3 hours before serving.

Apple-Coconut Cake

Makes 1 cake.

3½ cups unbleached flour
1 teaspoon baking soda
1 teaspoon salt
½ cup vegetable oil
3 eggs
¾ cup granulated sugar
2 teaspoons vanilla
½ cup skim milk
3 cups chopped or grated cooking apples
1½ cups coarsely chopped walnuts
½ cup grated coconut

Preheat oven to 350°. Combine flour, baking soda and salt; mix well. Combine oil, eggs, granulated sugar and vanilla. Alternately add flour mixture and milk until thoroughly blended. Fold in apples. Fold in nuts and coconut. Spread batter into a greased 9 x 13-inch baking pan. Bake 50 to 60 minutes or until cake tests done. Cool cake. Prepare Coconut Filling. Cut cake in half horizontally. Fill cake. Frost as desired.

Coconut Filling

4 egg yolks
2 eggs
⅓ cup granulated sugar
½ cup unbleached flour
¼ teaspoon salt
2 cups skim milk, scalded
1 teaspoon vanilla
½ teaspoon coconut extract

Place egg yolks, eggs and sugar in food processor or mixing bowl. Mix for 1 minute. Add flour and salt; mix 5 seconds. Slowly pour 1 cup of the milk into egg mixture, stirring constantly. Pour mixture into a saucepan along with remaining milk. Bring to a boil, stirring constantly, until thick. Remove from heat. Stir in vanilla and coconut extracts.

Yogurt Orange Sherbet

Makes 1 pint.

1 6-ounce can frozen orange juice concentrate
1 to 2 cups unflavored yogurt

Pour orange juice into a mixing bowl. Stir in yogurt to taste. Pour into freezer tray or bowl. Cover and freeze until serving time.

Pumpkin Bars

Makes 6 dozen.

1½ cups packed brown sugar
1¼ cups vegetable oil
4 eggs
2 cups canned pumpkin
1 cup unbleached flour
1 cup whole wheat flour
½ teaspoon salt
1 tablespoon cinnamon
2 teaspoons baking soda

Preheat oven to 350°. Blend sugar and oil. Beat in eggs until light. Add pumpkin and mix well. Combine dry ingredients. Gradually add to pumpkin mixture; mix thoroughly. Pour into a lightly greased jelly-roll pan. Bake 30 to 40 minutes or until top springs back when touched lightly in center. Cool on a wire rack. Frost with Cream Cheese Icing.

Cream Cheese Icing

1 8-ounce package cream cheese, at room temperature
6 tablespoons margarine, at room temperature
3 cups sifted confectioners' sugar
1 teaspoon vanilla

Cream cheese with margarine until light and fluffy. Gradually add sugar. Add vanilla. Beat until smooth and creamy.

Banana-Almond Cake

Makes 1 8-inch cake.

⅓ cup butter or margarine, at room temperature
¾ cup granulated sugar
3 eggs
2½ cups all-purpose flour
2 teaspoons baking powder
½ teaspoon salt
½ cup milk or buttermilk
3 ripe bananas, mashed
1 cup chopped walnuts
1 banana

Preheat oven to 350°. Cream together butter and sugar until light and fluffy. Add eggs and beat until light. Add remaining ingredients, in order, mixing well after each addition. Bake in 2 greased 8-inch cake pans for 50 to 60 minutes. Cool in pans placed on wire racks. Prepare Icing. Ice bottom layer. Slice banana and arrange on bottom layer. Add top layer. Spread cake with remaining icing.

Almond Icing

1 8-ounce package low-fat cream cheese, at room temperature
2 tablespoons butter, at room temperature
1 2-pound package confectioners' sugar, sifted
⅛ teaspoon salt
1 teaspoon almond extract

Cream together cheese and butter. Gradually add sugar, salt and almond extract. If icing is too thick, add a little water until it is of spreading consistency.

Buy bananas at discount prices. Peel, mash and freeze in one cup margarine containers.

Mc GUFFEY

FIRST
ECLECTI
READE

REVIS
EDIT

AMERICAN · BO
NEW YORK: CINC

Granola-Pumpkin Cookies

Makes 6 dozen.

1 cup margarine, at room temperature
¾ cup packed brown sugar
2 eggs
1 cup canned or cooked pumpkin, pureed
2 cups whole wheat pastry flour
¼ cup raw wheat germ
1 tablespoon baking powder
1 teaspoon salt
2 teaspoons allspice
1 teaspoon cinnamon
2 cups Granola (Recipe on page 13.)
1 teaspoon vanilla
½ cup raisins or currants
¼ cup chopped nuts

Preheat oven to 350°. Cream margarine and brown sugar. Add eggs and beat until light and fluffy. Stir in pumpkin. Sift together flour, wheat germ, baking powder, salt, allspice and cinnamon. Add to egg mixture. Stir in granola and vanilla. Stir in raisins and nuts. Drop by teaspoonfuls onto greased baking sheets. Bake 8 to 10 minutes or until lightly browned and top springs back when touched lightly. Cool on wire racks.

Lemon Tea Cakes

Makes 16.

1 cup unbleached flour
½ cup margarine
¼ cup confectioners' sugar
2 eggs
¾ cup granulated sugar
2 tablespoons unbleached flour
½ teaspoon baking powder
2 tablespoons lemon juice
Grated rind of 1 lemon
¼ teaspoon salt

Preheat oven to 350°. Combine flour, margarine and confectioners' sugar; mix thoroughly. Press into the bottom of an 8-inch square baking pan. Bake 15 minutes. Remove from oven, set aside to cool. Beat eggs until frothy. Gradually add sugar; beat until thick. Add remaining ingredients; mix well. Spread lemon mixture over crust. Bake for 25 minutes. The flavor improves if allowed to stand overnight before slicing. Cut into 2-inch squares.

Oatmeal Cookies

Makes 5 to 6 dozen.

1¾ cups packed brown sugar
1 cup margarine, at room temperature
2 eggs
2½ cups unbleached flour
½ cup raw wheat germ
½ cup bran flakes
2 teaspoons baking soda
2 teaspoons baking powder
2 teaspoons vanilla
2 cups old-fashioned oatmeal
⅔ cup chopped nuts and/or raisins
2 cups flaked coconut, optional

Preheat oven to 350°. Cream sugar with margarine. Add eggs and beat until light and fluffy. Combine flour, wheat germ, bran flakes, soda and baking powder; mix lightly. Add to egg mixture; mix well. Stir in vanilla, oatmeal, nuts and coconut. Roll dough into 1-inch balls. Place on greased baking sheets and flatten lightly with the floured bottom of a glass. Bake 8 to 10 minutes or until golden. Remove from baking sheets and cool on wire racks.

Candied Peel

Makes approximately 2 cups.

2 cups mixed grapefruit, orange, lime and lemon peel, cut into strips
1½ cups cold water
1 cup granulated sugar
½ cup water

Place mixed peel in a heavy saucepan. Cover with cold water. Bring slowly to a boil. Reduce heat and simmer 10 to 12 minutes; drain. Repeat 4 times or until peel is no longer bitter. Combine sugar and water in a small saucepan. Cook until thick and clear. Add peel. Boil gently until all syrup is absorbed and peel is transparent. Spread on wire racks to dry. Store in a tightly covered container.

Sesame Seed Cookies

Makes 3 dozen.

1¾ cups whole wheat flour
¼ cup soy flour
1 teaspoon baking powder
¼ teaspoon salt
¾ cup margarine, softened
¾ cup packed brown sugar
1 egg
2 tablespoons toasted sesame seed
1 tablespoon water
2 tablespoons raw sesame seed

Combine flours, baking powder and salt. Set aside. Cream margarine and sugar until light and fluffy. Add egg; beat until light. Stir in toasted sesame seed. Add flour and water to the egg mixture; mix well after each addition. Chill dough 3 to 4 hours. Drop dough by teaspoonfuls onto greased baking sheets. Flatten with a glass. Sprinkle on raw sesame seed. Bake at 375° 10 minutes, until edges are lightly browned.

Fresh Apple Fruitcake Cookies

Makes 4 dozen.

2½ cups whole wheat flour
¼ cup raw wheat germ
1 teaspoon baking soda
2 eggs, lightly beaten
2 cups raisins
2 cups grated apples
1 teaspoon cinnamon
⅛ teaspoon cloves
¼ teaspoon nutmeg
½ teaspoon ginger
2 cups Candied Peel (Recipe on page 59.)
½ cup chopped nuts
1 14-ounce can sweetened condensed milk

Preheat oven to 350°. Combine flour, wheat germ and baking soda; mix well. Combine eggs, raisins, apples, spices, peel, nuts and sweetened condensed milk; mix well. Add dry ingredients and mix well. Drop by teaspoonfuls onto well-greased baking sheets. Bake for 10 minutes or until golden. To store, sprinkle with orange or apple juice or brandy. Keep in a tightly covered container in a cool place.

Carob Cake

Makes 6 to 8 servings.

Note: Have all ingredients at room temperature.

1½ cups sifted unbleached flour
1½ teaspoons baking powder
½ teaspoon salt
½ cup granulated sugar
2 tablespoons carob powder
1 stick margarine or butter
2 eggs
3 tablespoons milk
½ cup chopped walnuts

Preheat oven to 375°. Combine dry ingredients in a large mixing bowl. Add remaining ingredients, except walnuts, and beat at high speed for 2 minutes. Stir in walnuts. Pour into a greased 8- or 9-inch cake pan. Bake for 30 minutes, or until cake tests done. Cool cake and ice.

Carob Icing

1 stick butter or margarine
1 to 2 tablespoons carob powder (to taste)
1¼ cups confectioners' sugar
1 teaspoon vanilla
¼ cup chopped walnuts

Place all ingredients, except nuts, in a medium-size bowl. Beat until light and fluffy. Sprinkle chopped nuts on top.

Carrot Cookies

Makes 6 dozen.

2 cups unbleached flour
¼ cup raw wheat germ
½ teaspoon baking powder
½ teaspoon baking soda
¼ teaspoon salt
1 cup margarine, at room temperature
¾ cup firmly packed brown sugar
2 eggs
1 teaspoon vanilla
1 teaspoon grated orange rind
2 cups rolled oats
1 cup grated carrots
1 cup chopped nuts
⅔ cup flaked or shredded coconut

Preheat oven to 350°. Combine the first 5 ingredients in a mixing bowl. In a separate bowl, cream margarine and brown sugar until smooth. Add eggs and beat until light and fluffy. Add vanilla; mix well. Gradually add flour mixture, mixing thoroughly. Stir in remaining ingredients. Drop by teaspoonfuls onto greased baking sheets. Bake for 12 minutes, or until lightly browned.

Raw sugar has no more nutritional benefits than refined white sugar. For added nutrition, try substituting molasses or honey for refined sugar whenever possible.

Pfeffernusse

Makes 10 dozen.

2 cups whole wheat flour
2 cups unbleached flour
½ teaspoon salt
1 teaspoon baking soda
2 teaspoons cinnamon
¼ teaspoon allspice
¼ teaspoon ground cloves
½ teaspoon cardamom
1 tablespoon anise seed, crushed
1 cup butter or margarine
1 cup packed brown sugar
2 eggs
1 cup old-fashioned molasses
1 cup chopped nuts
¾ pound seedless raisins, chopped or ground

Combine dry ingredients, except nuts and raisins; mix thoroughly. Cream together butter and sugar until light and fluffy. Add eggs and beat until light. Stir in molasses. Gradually add dry ingredients; mix well. Stir in nuts and raisins. Refrigerate overnight. Preheat oven to 350°. Roll dough into small balls and place them on lightly greased baking sheets. Bake 11 minutes or until golden. Store in airtight containers.

Whole Wheat Cookies

Makes approximately 3 dozen.

2 cups whole wheat flour
¼ cup firmly packed brown sugar
⅔ cup butter or margarine
1 egg, beaten
½ teaspoon vanilla

Preheat oven to 350°. Place flour and sugar in a medium-size mixing bowl. Cut in butter with a pastry blender or fork until mixture resembles crumbs. Add egg and vanilla and mix to make a stiff dough. Roll out on a floured surface. Cut into rounds with a cookie or biscuit cutter. Place on greased baking sheets. Bake 20 minutes, or until golden.

Date Nut Bars

Makes 12 to 16 bars.

¼ cup margarine or butter
⅔ cup firmly packed brown sugar
2 eggs
¾ cup whole wheat flour
¼ cup raw wheat germ
½ teaspoon baking powder
½ teaspoon salt
1¼ cups chopped dates
½ cup chopped nuts
½ teaspoon vanilla

Preheat oven to 350°. Cream margarine and sugar until light and fluffy. Add eggs and beat until light and fluffy. Combine dry ingredients in a separate bowl and mix lightly. Gradually add dry ingredients and mix thoroughly. Stir in remaining ingredients; mix well. Pour into a greased 9-inch baking pan. Bake for 30 minutes, or until the top springs back when lightly touched. Cut into squares while still warm.

Glorified Rice Pudding

Makes 8 servings.

1½ cups cooked rice
2 egg yolks, well beaten
⅓ cup honey
1 cup crushed pineapple, drained
1 tablespoon cornstarch
1 tablespoon lemon juice
2 egg whites

Preheat oven to 350°. Combine rice, yolks, honey, pineapple, cornstarch and lemon juice; mix well. Beat egg whites until stiff but not dry. Fold egg whites into rice mixture. Spoon mixture into a buttered 1½-quart casserole. Bake for 30 minutes or until puffed and browned.

Carrot Pudding

Makes 6 servings.

1 pound carrots, sliced
1 cup milk
½ cup non-instant powdered milk
3 eggs, lightly beaten
⅓ cup packed brown sugar
1 teaspoon grated lemon rind
½ teaspoon allspice
¾ teaspoon cinnamon
¾ teaspoon nutmeg
⅛ teaspoon salt

Steam carrots until tender. Preheat oven to 350°. Place carrots, milk and powdered milk in blender; pureé. Add remaining ingredients and mix thoroughly. Pour into six lightly greased custard or tea cups that hold at least ⅔ cup. Place custard cups in a shallow baking pan. Pour 1 inch boiling water into pan. Bake 35 to 40 minutes or until knife inserted in center comes out clean. Serve warm or cool.

Bread Pudding

Makes 6 servings.

1½ to 2 cups dry, whole wheat bread cubes
   Water
2 eggs
3 cups milk
⅓ cup honey
¼ cup raw wheat germ
¼ cup non-instant powdered milk
¼ teaspoon salt
½ teaspoon cinnamon
1 teaspoon vanilla
½ cup raisins or currants
½ cup chopped nuts, optional

Butter a 1½- or 2-quart, flat, baking dish. Place bread cubes in the bottom. Preheat oven to 350°. Bring a saucepan of water to a boil. In a large bowl, beat eggs until light and foamy. Add milk, honey, wheat germ, powdered milk, salt, cinnamon and vanilla; blend well. Pour over bread cubes. Let stand until bread absorbs liquid. Sprinkle raisins and nuts over the top of the pudding. Place baking dish into a larger, flat pan. Fill outer pan halfway with hot water. Bake for 1 hour uncovered until firm, or a knife inserted in center comes out almost clean. May be served hot or cold.

Mix yogurt with nuts and chopped fruit. Freeze in paper drinking cups with wooden sticks inserted in the middle. When frozen, peel off paper and eat as you would ice cream.

BEVERAGES

Beverages and snacks can be a healthful part of the diet. Try these recipes for beverages containing milk and juices which help fulfill dietary considerations. And, snacks that are made of naturally nutritious ingredients are a plus in any diet.

AND SNACKS

Orange Pep-Up

Makes 3 cups.

- 1 cup chilled orange juice
- 1 cup cold milk
- 1 cup sliced carrots
- ¼ cup non-instant powdered milk
- 1 to 3 teaspoons nutritional yeast
- ¼ cup toasted wheat germ
  Honey, optional
- 2 ice cubes

Place all ingredients, except ice cubes, in blender or food processor. With blender on high, drop in ice cubes and blend until mixture is smooth.

Hot Apple Cider

Makes 8 cups.

- ½ gallon apple cider
- ¼ teaspoon ground allspice
- ¾ teaspoon grated orange rind
- 1 cinnamon stick
- 2 cardamom seeds, or ⅛ teaspoon ground
- 6 whole cloves
  Orange slices, studded with cloves, optional

Combine all ingredients, except orange slices, in a large, heavy saucepan. Cover and bring to a boil. Reduce heat and simmer 15 minutes. Taste and correct seasonings. Strain before serving. Garnish with orange slices.

Skim Buttermilk

Makes 4½ cups.

- 4 cups skim milk, at room temperature
- ½ cup fresh buttermilk, at room temperature

Combine skim milk and buttermilk. Pour into a sterile, 5-cup jar. Let stand until buttermilk is clabbered. Stir until smooth and refrigerate. May be used in any recipe calling for buttermilk or sour milk.

Super Juice

Makes 5 cups.

- 3½ cups chopped tomatoes
- ½ cup chopped celery
- ¼ cup chopped onion
- ⅓ cup chopped carrot
- ½ cup chopped green pepper
- ½ cup chopped cucumber
- ¼ cup chopped parsley
- ¼ cup water
  Salt, optional
  Freshly ground black pepper
  Fresh dill, optional

Place all ingredients, except salt, pepper and dill into a large heavy saucepan. Bring to a boil, reduce heat, cover and simmer 10 minutes. Cool thoroughly. Place in blender; puree. Add seasonings to taste. Chill and garnish with dill, if desired.

Hot Honey and Lemon Drink

Makes 1 cup.

- 1½ tablespoons lemon juice
- 2 tablespoons honey
- 1 cup boiling water

Place lemon juice and honey in a large mug. Pour boiling water over; mix well.

Banana Blend

Makes 2⅔ cups.

- 2 cups cold milk
- 2 tablespoons peanut butter
- 3 tablespoons toasted wheat germ
- 1 banana, sliced in thirds
- 1 ice cube

Place all ingredients, except ice cube, in blender or food processor. With blender on high, drop in ice cube and blend until mixture is smooth.

Apple Limeade

Makes 1¼ cups.

- 1 cup unsweetened apple juice
- 1 tablespoon lime juice
- ½ cup crushed ice
  Lime slice

Place all ingredients, except lime, in a covered jar or in a shaker. Shake well. Garnish with lime slice.

Tomato Juice

Makes 6 cups.

10 to 12 ripe tomatoes, chopped
¼ cup chopped onion
¼ cup chopped celery
¼ bay leaf, crumbled
¼ cup chopped parsley
1 teaspoon salt, optional
⅛ teaspoon black pepper
¼ teaspoon brown sugar

Place tomatoes, vegetables, bay leaf and parsley in a large saucepan. Bring to a boil. Reduce heat, cover and simmer until tomatoes are tender, stirring often. Remove from heat and cool. Puree in a blender or press through a sieve. Add salt, pepper and brown sugar. Chill before serving.

Raspberry Frosty

Makes 2 cups.

1 cup frozen raspberries
1 tablespoon orange juice
1 cup milk
   Honey, optional
2 or more ice cubes

Place raspberries, orange juice and milk in a blender container. Cover and blend. Taste and add honey, if necessary. With blender on high, drop in ice cubes 1 at a time, and blend until smooth.

Cantaloupe Flip

Makes 2 cups.

½ cup unflavored yogurt
½ cubed cantaloupe
½ cup cold milk
1 teaspoon lemon juice
   Honey, optional
2 ice cubes

Place all ingredients, except ice cubes, in blender container. With blender on high, drop in ice cubes and blend until smooth.

Carrot Juice

Makes 3 cups.

3 medium carrots, grated or shredded
2 cups water
⅓ cup non-instant powdered milk

Place carrots and water in a medium saucepan. Cover tightly and bring to a boil. Reduce heat and simmer ½ hour or until carrots are tender. Cool. Place carrot mixture in a blender along with powdered milk; blend until smooth.

Purple Cow

Makes 1½ cups.

1 cup milk
½ cup unsweetened grape juice
½ cup crushed ice

Place all ingredients in a blender container. Cover and blend until smooth.

Carob Milk

Makes 1½ cups.

1 cup cold milk
1 tablespoon carob powder
1 teaspoon honey
¼ teaspoon vanilla
2 ice cubes

Place all ingredients, except ice cubes, in blender container. With blender on high, drop in ice cubes and blend until mixture is frothy.

Blue Moon

Makes 1½ cups.

1 cup evaporated milk
1 cup fresh blueberries
   Honey, optional
¼ teaspoon vanilla
3 ice cubes

Place all ingredients, except ice cubes, in blender container. With blender on high, drop in ice cubes and blend until smooth.

Strawberry Milk

Makes 2⅔ cups.

2 cups cold milk
1 cup frozen strawberries
1 teaspoon lemon juice
   Honey, optional
2 ice cubes
   Fresh strawberries

Place all ingredients, except ice cubes, in blender or food processor. With blender on high, drop in ice cubes and blend until smooth. Garnish with fresh strawberries.

Orange Drink

Makes 3 cups.

1 6-ounce can frozen, concentrated orange juice
1 cup milk
1 cup water
1 teaspoon vanilla
10 ice cubes

Combine all ingredients, except ice cubes, in blender container. Blend on high, dropping in ice cubes one at a time, until all cubes are liquified. If desired, serve this drink topped with a scoop of vanilla ice cream.

Yogurt Dip

Makes 3 cups.

1 medium tomato, chopped
3 tablespoons lemon juice
½ teaspoon salt
   Freshly ground black pepper
¼ teaspoon Worcestershire sauce
½ cup minced scallions
2 cups unflavored yogurt
   Minced chives

Marinate tomato in lemon juice for 1 hour. Add remaining ingredients, except chives. Mix lightly. Garnish top with chives.

Spinach-Stuffed Mushrooms

Makes 6 to 8 servings.

- 1 pound mushrooms
- ½ cup butter or margarine
- 1 tablespoon minced onion
- 1 10-ounce package frozen spinach, cooked and drained
  Nutmeg to taste
  Salt and pepper to taste, optional
- ⅓ cup grated Cheddar cheese

Clean mushrooms. Remove stems; chop. Heat half of the butter in a saucepan. Add chopped mushrooms and onion; sauté until onion is tender. Remove from pan and set aside. Add remaining butter to saucepan. Gently and quickly sauté mushroom caps. Drain on absorbent paper. Place spinach, onion and chopped mushrooms in a blender container. Add seasonings. Puree. Fill mushroom caps with mixture. Sprinkle with grated cheese. Place on baking sheets and bake at 375° for 15 minutes.

Salmon Ball

Makes 6 servings.

- 1 16-ounce can red salmon, drained and flaked
- 1 8-ounce package cream cheese, softened
- 1 small onion, finely chopped
- 2 tablespoons lemon juice
- ½ cup minced parsley
- ¼ cup chopped nuts

Combine salmon and cream cheese; blend thoroughly. Add onion and lemon juice and mix well. Shape into a ball. Wrap in waxed paper; refrigerate until firm. Sprinkle parsley and nuts on waxed paper; mix thoroughly. Roll salmon ball in nut mixture and coat thoroughly. Refrigerate until serving time.

Seed and Nut Spread

Makes 2 cups.

- 1 cup raw sunflower seeds
- 1 cup untoasted sesame seeds
- 2 cups cashews, pecans, walnuts or almonds
  Vegetable oil
  Honey, optional

Place seeds and nuts in a food processor or blender and finely chop. Add oil a little at a time and blend to a spreading consistency. If desired, add a small amount of honey. Store upside down in a tightly covered jar, in the refrigerator. Use to stuff celery, as a vegetable dip or as a sandwich spread.

Serve your family unsweetened fruit juices such as orange, grapefruit, apple, grape and similar fruit juices. They are made from fully ripened fruits which are at the peak of natural sweetness.

Soy Nuts

Makes 2 cups.

- 1 cup dry soybeans
- 3 cups cold water
- ¼ cup vegetable oil
  Salt, garlic powder, chili powder, garlic salt or onion salt

Soak soybeans in water overnight. Bring to a boil; reduce heat, cover and simmer for 30 minutes. Remove cover and cool. Heat oil in a large frying pan. Add soybeans and fry until golden, stirring regularly. Remove from heat. Sprinkle on your choice of seasonings. Eat as a snack or use as garnish on top of casseroles, salads and sandwiches.

Wheat Germ Crackers

Makes about 2 dozen.

- 1 cup whole wheat pastry flour
- ½ cup unbleached flour
- 2 tablespoons soy flour
- 2 teaspoons baking powder
- ¾ cup raw wheat germ
- ¼ teaspoon salt
- ½ cup margarine
- 1 tablespoon brown sugar
- 2 tablespoons milk
- 1 egg white, lightly beaten
  Raw wheat germ

Combine first 6 ingredients; mix lightly. Cut in margarine until mixture resembles coarse crumbs. Add brown sugar, milk and egg white. Mix lightly with a fork. Shape into a ball. Preheat oven to 400°. Roll out dough on a well-floured board to about ⅛-inch thickness. Cut dough with a round cookie cutter. Sprinkle tops of dough with wheat germ. Bake on ungreased baking sheets for 6 minutes or until golden.

Cheese Ball

Makes 3 cups.

- 8 ounces sharp Cheddar cheese, grated
- 1 8-ounce package cream cheese, softened
- 8 ounces processed American cheese, grated
- 2 tablespoons Worcestershire sauce
- ⅛ teaspoon onion salt
- ⅛ teaspoon garlic salt
- ⅛ teaspoon celery salt
- ⅛ teaspoon paprika
- 1 to 2 cups chopped soy nuts

Combine all ingredients, except nuts, in a mixing bowl; cream well. Shape into a ball. Wrap and chill until serving time. Roll in nuts.

FOR BABIES AND TODDLERS

When the time comes to introduce solids into your baby's diet, try some of these recipes for making the food yourself. Included are recipes for simple foods, such as cereal and rice, as well as recipes that the older baby will enjoy along with the rest of the family. Also included are suggestions for finger foods and snacks for the toddler set.

A baby's primary source of nutrition for the first year of life is mother's milk or fortified formula. From a nutritional standpoint, solids are unnecessary during the first three months of life. Before this time, a baby's ability to chew is not totally developed. So never rush a baby into eating solid food and don't be alarmed if your baby rejects or spits out solids that are offered before that time.

There does come a time, however, when baby is ready to eat and enjoy all kinds of foods. Somewhere between the third and sixth month, the baby will show signs of developmental readiness. This is evidenced by the baby's response to a spoon and the ability of the tongue and swallowing mechanism to deal with nonliquids.

When you do introduce solids into baby's diet, it is generally advised to begin with cereal, such as rice, and fruit—most commonly strained banana or applesauce.

Start by offering a spoonful or less until baby is used to the taste. Offer it several times over a period of three or four days, watching for signs of an allergy, such as hives, diarrhea, gas, general discomfort, restlessness or crying from 20 minutes to 1 hour after eating. This is especially significant if any of these signs occur after the second exposure to a particular food.

Introduce only one new food at a time, and only one a week. This way, if the baby is allergic to a particular food, it will be easier to identify.

After introducing cereals and fruits, gradually add the green vegetables and then yellow vegetables, following your pediatrician's advice as to when they should be included. The first meat to be given to babies is generally chicken, since it is more easily digested than other meats.

Do not force a baby to eat more than she wants. Babies have the capacity of letting you know when to stop. Heed the warning. There is no advantage in overfeeding a baby. In fact, recent studies indicate that obesity in later life may often begin in the first months of life. Remember, love is not measured by the amount of food your baby is fed.

How to Make Baby Food

Making baby food at home is a simple procedure that can be incorporated into planning your family meals. All you need is something in which to puree the food, such as a blender, food processor, food mill or even a small, inexpensive baby food grinder.

When serving baby a part of the family meal, remove baby's portion before adding seasonings, especially salt and sugar. Then puree.

As the baby becomes accustomed to eating solids and becomes proficient enough to handle a lumpier consistency, the food can be more coarsely ground or mashed.

Before preparing baby's food, thoroughly clean all utensils in hot, soapy water and rinse well.

When feeding baby, remove only a small portion of the food at a time and feed the baby from that. Any food the baby has only partially eaten should be thrown away. The reserved portion will not be contaminated.

Baby food may be frozen and

Chicken Noodle Soup, 76

reheated as needed. There are a couple of easy ways to freeze food. One way is to place spoonfuls of prepared food on a baking sheet lined with foil and freeze quickly. Remove the frozen food from the sheet and store in a tightly sealed container. Another method is to place the food in plastic ice cube trays. When the food is frozen, pop it out of the tray and store the "food cubes" for later use. Reheat in a warming dish or place the cubes in a container and heat in a pan of warm water.

Although a baby can learn to eat almost anything an adult might eat, there are certain things which should be avoided, since they are hard to digest and/or may cause choking or gagging. Following is a list of foods which are generally not advisable to feed a baby under the age of fifteen to eighteen months:

Bacon
Baked beans
Carrot sticks
Celery sticks
Chocolate
Corn
Cucumbers
Leafy vegetables, such as lettuce and uncooked spinach
Olives
Onions
Nuts
Popcorn
Potato chips

Following is a list of foods which you might like to offer baby during the ages given:

From 6 to 8 months
Applesauce
Arrowroot cookies
Cottage Cheese
Bananas, mashed or sliced for finger food

Graham crackers
Mashed potatoes
Yogurt
Cooked Cereals
Vegetables, steamed and mashed
Gelatin

From 9 to 12 months
Even without a mouth full of teeth baby is ready to chew. Start offering more finger foods. And, prepare baby for totally solid food by making pureed or mashed foods a little lumpier so that baby will become accustomed to it.

Apples, oranges, peaches, peeled and cut into pieces
Soft cheese cut into small pieces
Pasta, such as macaroni and noodles
Rice
Boneless fish
Tiny meatballs
Eggs, boiled, scrambled or poached

From 12 months and up
Halved cherry tomatoes
Mushrooms
Avocado, cut in pieces
Asparagus tips
Broccoli tips
French fries
Pickle spears
Hard-boiled eggs
Fruit cocktail
Watermelon, seeded and cut into pieces
Cantaloupe, cut into pieces
Beef frankfurters
Ham, cut into small pieces
Tuna fish
Hamburger
Oyster crackers
Bagels and cream cheese
Spinach noodles

Baby Joins the Family
Mealtime is important for the family. It is a time when everyone joins to share a part of their day. Children will integrate into family mealtime more easily if nudged in that direction by a little help from their parents.

Following are suggestions to make mealtime a pleasant experience:

- A quiet time before meals allows the child to slow down before eating and helps to make mealtime a pleasant, unhurried experience.
- The parents' positive attitude about the foods they eat builds good habits by their example.
- Encourage children to self-feed by giving them easy-to-use utensils—spoons and forks should have short, straight handles; cups should be broad-mouthed and easy to hold.
- Use easy-to-clean, durable materials for floors, tabletops, and table coverings. Accidents occur as children learn their new skills, but don't let accidents at the table take the fun out of mealtime.
- Children are greatly encouraged by bright colors and textures. Offer foods such as carrots, peas, strawberries; crunchy foods such as raw vegetables, crackers or pieces of apple. Smooth, cool foods are always a favorite.
- Do not force a child to eat. It may destroy her natural acceptance of food. A casual attitude toward how much she eats is more advantageous in the long run. Teach your child that eating is not a chore, but something to be enjoyed.
- Serve child-size servings. It's far better to pass out second helpings than discard uneaten food. And, it creates less stress on the child.

RECOMMENDATIONS FOR THE KINDS AND AMOUNTS OF FOOD TO BE CONSUMED AT SPECIFIC STAGES DURING INFANCY

AGE	DEVELOPMENTAL STAGE	FOOD AND AMOUNTS* CONSUMED DAILY
0-3 months	Sucks & swallows liquids; tongue protrusion reflex is predominant; head-bobbing.	Breast milk or iron-fortified infant formula only
4-6 months	Sits with minimal support; head is erect and steady; can transfer food from front of tongue to back of mouth and swallows non-liquid food.	Breast milk or iron-fortified infant formula Dry infant cereal (up to 8 tablespoons) If breast-fed, give strained meats (3-4 tablespoons) If bottle-fed, give strained fruits and vegetables (up to 8 tablespoons) Juice (2-4 ounces)
7-9 months	Sits unsupported, balances head well and has body control; able to mash food with jaw and swallow food of different textures and consistency; begins self-feeding.	Breast milk or iron-fortified infant formula Dry infant cereal (8-12 tablespoons) Strained to finely chopped fruits and vegetables (6-8 tablespoons) Juice (2-4 ounces) Strained to ground meats (2 to 4 tablespoons) Toast or teething biscuit
10-12 months	Continues increasing skill in biting, chewing and swallowing food; holds cup, uses spoon and likes self-feeding.	Breast milk or iron-fortified infant formula or whole milk** Dry infant cereal (8-12 tablespoons) Fork-mashed or soft fruits and cooked vegetables (6-8 tablespoons) Juice (2-4 ounces) Ground or chopped meat and substitutes (1-2 ounces) Potato and whole grain or enriched grain products Toast or teething biscuits

* Amounts of formula vary based on energy and growth needs. Amounts for breast milk are not easily identified; supply is usually based on demand.

** Vitamin D fortified whole cow milk can be used when combined with iron sources of high biological availability and sufficient solid food to balance protein, fat and carbohydrates.

Adapted from "Basic Nutrition Facts," courtesy of the Michigan Department of Public Health.

Recipes on pages 70 and 72 make 1 baby-size serving.

Fruit and Cereal Combo

Cream of Rice, Cream of Wheat, or oatmeal, cooked
Pureed fruit, such as apples, apricots, bananas, or peaches

Spoon fruit over cereal.

Oatmeal and Banana

¼ cup rolled oats
¾ cup water, formula or milk
⅓ ripe banana, pureed or mashed

Combine oats and ½ cup of the water or milk. Bring to a boil. Cover and cook over low heat for 5 minutes, stirring constantly. Remove from heat. Let stand, covered, for 5 minutes. Combine remaining milk with banana; mix thoroughly. Stir banana into cereal.

Apple-Honey Yogurt

2 cups chopped, ripe apple
¼ cup seedless raisins
2 tablespoons apple juice
½ cup unflavored yogurt
Honey as needed

Place apples, raisins and juice in a small saucepan. Cover and cook over low heat until apples are tender. Cool and puree, if necessary. Blend honey and yogurt together. Stir in apple mixture. Serve cool.

Spinach

½ tablespoon butter
2 tablespoons water
½ cup fresh spinach

Melt butter in a small saucepan. Add water. Add spinach. Cook for 1 minute or until tender. Puree and serve.

Mashed Potato and Spinach

1 small potato
1 cup spinach, torn into bite-size pieces
1 to 2 tablespoons milk
½ teaspoon butter

Pare potato; dice. Cook potato in ½ cup boiling water until tender; drain. Add spinach and cook until tender. Add more water if necessary. Combine potato, spinach, milk and butter in blender. Puree.

Green Beans, Zucchini or Turnips

¼ cup sliced vegetable
½ tablespoon butter or margarine

Steam vegetable until tender. Drain. Place in blender container along with butter. Puree. If too thick, add a small amount of milk.

Cottage Cheese and Fruit

½ cup cottage cheese
½ cup fresh, cooked or uncooked fruit
4 to 6 tablespoons apple or orange juice
2 teaspoons honey, optional

Place cottage cheese and fruit in a blender container. Blend well. Stir in juice until desired consistency. If fruit is too tart, add honey.

Creamed Cauliflower

¼ cup cauliflowerets
½ slice American cheese
½ tablespoon butter

Steam cauliflower until tender. Drain. Mash with a fork or puree. Combine cheese and butter in a saucepan, melt over low heat. Stir into cauliflower.

All-in-One Stew

2 ounces lean ground beef
1 small potato, cubed and cooked
¼ cup green beans, cooked
2 tablespoons milk

Broil beef. Combine beef, potato, beans and milk in blender container. Puree. Add more milk, if necessary.

Toddler French Bread

1 slice thin whole wheat bread
1 egg, beaten
1 teaspoon butter

Soak bread in egg until egg is absorbed. Melt butter in a small frying pan. Fry bread until lightly browned on both sides. Cut into fingers and cool.

Fish and Egg Breakfast

1 egg
1 teaspoon milk
2 teaspoons butter or margarine
¼ cup flaked, poached white fish, skin and bones removed

Combine egg and milk and mix thoroughly. Melt butter in a small frying pan. Pour egg mixture into pan. Gently stir in fish. Stir eggs and cook until done.

Potatoes au Gratin, 72

american baby

MARCH 1980

FOR EXPECTANT AND NEW PARENTS

WHEN THERE'S MORE THAN ONE
The joys and challenges of raising twins

Turkey-Topped Potato

4 tablespoons water
¼ cup cubed, cooked turkey
1 tablespoon butter or
  margarine
1 teaspoon flour
¼ cup milk
¼ cup mashed potato

Place water and turkey in blender container; blend well. Combine butter and flour in a small pan. Cook over low heat for 2 minutes, stirring constantly. Gradually stir in milk. Cook until thickened, stirring constantly. Add turkey and heat through. Spoon over potato.

Pork Stew

¼ cup cubed, cooked pork
½ sweet potato, cooked
¼ cup milk
3 green beans, cooked
⅓ carrot, cooked

Combine pork, potato and milk in a blender container. Blend until smooth. Add beans and carrot. Pulse blender to lightly chop vegetables. Heat mixture in a saucepan before serving.

Chicken and Pear Souffle

1 teaspoon flour
1 tablespoon butter or
  margarine
¼ cup milk
¼ cup diced, cooked chicken
2 tablespoons diced pear
1 egg yolk, lightly beaten

Combine flour and butter in a pan and cook over low heat for 2 minutes, stirring constantly. Gradually stir in milk. Cook until mixture thickens, stirring constantly. Add chicken, pear and egg yolk. Simmer for 1 minute. Pour into a lightly greased baking dish. Bake at 350° for 35 minutes.

Creamy Asparagus

4 asparagus tips, cleaned
1 tablespoon butter or
  margarine
1 teaspoon flour
¼ cup milk
½ egg yolk

Steam the asparagus until tender. Drain. Combine butter, flour, milk and egg yolk; mix well. Cook over low heat until thickened, stirring constantly. Add asparagus; heat through.

Chicken and Peas

¼ cup diced, cooked chicken
⅛ cup cooked peas
¼ small tomato, peeled

Place all ingredients in a blender container. Blend well. Thin with a small amount of milk, if necessary. Spoon into a lightly greased baking dish. Bake at 350° for 20 minutes.

Instead of using powdered or canned fruit drinks for babies, use the more nutritious fresh or frozen fruit juices.

Potatoes au Gratin

½ medium potato, peeled and
  diced
1 tablespoon butter or
  margarine
¼ cup milk
2 tablespoons grated
  Parmesan cheese

Place potatoes in a small, greased baking dish. Add milk. Sprinkle cheese over top. Bake at 375° for 15 minutes or until potatoes are tender.

Apricot Omelet

1 egg, lightly beaten
1 apricot, peeled, pitted and
  minced
2 tablespoons butter or
  margarine

Combine egg and apricot; mix lightly. Melt butter in a small frying pan. Add egg and cook until set, lifting edges to allow uncooked portion to flow underneath.

Ham and Cheese Omelet

1 egg, lightly beaten
2 tablespoons grated Swiss
  cheese
2 tablespoons minced cooked
  ham
2 tablespoons butter or
  margarine

Combine egg, cheese and ham; mix lightly. Melt butter in a small frying pan over low heat. Pour in egg mixture and cook until set, lifting edges to allow uncooked portion to flow underneath.

Chicken and Rice Stew

1 cup cubed, cooked chicken
¼ cup cooked rice
¼ cup cooked peas, sliced
  carrots or cut green beans
¼ cup chicken broth
¼ cup milk

Place all ingredients in a blender container. Blend well. Heat through before serving.

Ground Beef Stew

¼ cup ground beef, broiled
4 green beans, cooked
¼ small tomato, peeled
½ boiled potato, diced

Place beef, green beans and tomato in a blender container. Blend well. Spoon into a small greased casserole. Sprinkle potato on top. Bake at 350° for 15 minutes.

Granola Bars

Makes 16 bars.

- ½ cup firmly packed brown sugar
- ½ cup margarine or butter
- ½ cup rolled oats
- ½ cup whole wheat flour
- ½ cup unbleached flour
- ¼ cup raw wheat germ
- 1 teaspoon cinnamon
- ½ teaspoon allspice
- 2 eggs, lightly beaten
- 2 cups Granola or Pruneola (Recipes on page 13)
- ¼ cup chopped nuts or coconut
- 2 tablespoons brown sugar

Preheat oven to 350°. Cream together margarine and sugar. Stir in oats, flours, wheat germ and spices. Pack into a lightly greased 8-inch baking pan. Combine eggs, granola, nuts, and brown sugar; mix well. Pour over oat mixture; spread evenly. Bake 30 minutes or until lightly golden. Cool; cut into 2-inch bars.

Cheese Croquettes

Makes 4 servings.

- 1 cup grated Monterey Jack cheese
- ½ cup dry bread crumbs
- 1 tablespoon butter
- 1 egg
- ½ teaspoon bottled steak sauce
- ¼ teaspoon ground sweet basil
- ¼ teaspoon ground thyme
  Paprika
  Salt and pepper to taste, optional

Combine all ingredients in a mixing bowl. Stir until well blended. Form into croquettes, balls or patties. Fry in 375° oil until golden brown.

Peanutty Oatmeal Snack

Makes 16 bars.

- 2 cups rolled oats
- ⅓ cup milk
- ⅓ cup crunchy peanut butter
- ½ cup honey
- ⅓ cup nonfat dry milk
- ⅓ cup raisins
- ½ cup mixed seeds or toasted wheat germ

Preheat oven to 350°. Spread rolled oats on a baking sheet; toast for 15 minutes or until golden. Combine milk, peanut butter and honey in a small saucepan. Bring mixture to a boil; remove from heat. Add raisins, seeds or wheat germ and dry milk. Stir in toasted oats. Press mixture firmly into an 8-inch square pan. Chill for 1 hour. Cut into 2-inch squares. Mixture may also be rolled into small balls and chilled. Store in refrigerator.

Pocket Bread French Toast

Makes 4 servings.

- 2 eggs
- 1 tablespoon milk
- 2 tablespoons margarine or butter
- 4 medium-sized pocket bread

Beat eggs and milk together thoroughly. Heat margarine in a large frying pan. Soak pocket bread on both sides in the egg mixture; place in frying pan. Fry until golden brown and puffy; turn. Fry on the other side until golden.

Cream of Fruit Soup

Makes 4 to 6 servings.

- 2 pears, peeled and seeded
- 4 apricots, peeled and seeded
- 3 peaches, peeled and seeded
- 3 cups milk

Cut all fruit into 1-inch chunks. Place in blender container and blend until smooth. Slowly blend in milk. Pour mixture into a saucepan. Heat slowly for about 10 minutes. May also be served cold, garnished with a dollop of yogurt.

It is unnecessary to add either sugar or salt to a baby's food. Natural salts and sugars in foods are enough seasoning for a young child.

Yogurt Chicken

Makes 4 to 5 servings.

- 3½ pounds chicken, cut-up or 4 chicken breasts, split
- 1 teaspoon paprika
  Freshly ground black pepper
- 3 tablespoons whole wheat flour
- 3 tablespoons margarine
- ½ cup orange juice
- 1 cup chicken broth
- 1 cup unflavored yogurt

Wash chicken pieces and pat dry. Combine seasonings and flour in a paper bag. Drop in chicken, one piece at a time, and shake bag to coat chicken. Melt margarine in a frying pan and lightly brown chicken. Reduce heat, pour orange juice and chicken broth over chicken. Cover and simmer 45 minutes or until chicken is tender. Remove from heat. Push chicken to one side. Add yogurt, and stir to make a sauce. Remove the baby's portion of the chicken and discard skin and bones. Chop or puree the chicken. Place remaining chicken in a serving dish and spoon sauce over.

Peanut Butter Balls

Makes 2 dozen.

⅓ cup honey
½ cup crunchy, old-fashioned peanut butter
¼ cup raisins
¼ cup raw sunflower seeds
¾ cup non-instant, non-fat dry milk

Blend together honey, peanut butter, raisins and sunflower seeds. Gradually stir in dry milk until mixture is thoroughly blended. Divide into balls and chill until firm.

Honey Graham Crackers

Makes 2 dozen.

1 cup graham flour
1 cup unbleached flour
1 teaspoon salt
1 teaspoon baking powder
¼ cup butter or margarine
½ cup honey
¼ cup milk

Combine dry ingredients in a mixing bowl; mix lightly. Cut in butter until mixture is the consistency of coarse crumbs. Stir in honey and mix well. Gradually stir in milk to make a stiff dough. Turn out onto a floured surface. Roll out with a floured rolling pin to ¼-inch thickness. Use a sharp knife to cut dough into 3-inch squares. Prick with a fork. Bake on ungreased baking sheets for about 18 minutes or until golden brown.

Banapple Drink

1 small apple
2 tablespoons pureed banana

Peel apple and cut into chunks. Place in a blender container and blend well. Add a small amount of apple juice, if too thick. Stir in banana.

Apricot-Honey Drink

Makes 6 servings.

½ cup dried apricots
2 cups unsweetened pineapple juice
½ cup honey
½ cup orange juice
3 tablespoons lemon juice
1 3.3-ounce can evaporated milk

Soak apricots in pineapple juice until softened. Place in a blender container; blend until smooth. Add remaining ingredients and blend well. Chill before serving.

Whole Wheat Cookies

Makes 5 to 6 dozen.

1½ cups firmly packed brown sugar
3 cups rolled oats
1½ cups white flour
1½ cups whole wheat flour
¾ teaspoon baking soda
3 sticks margarine

Preheat oven to 350°. Combine dry ingredients in a large mixing bowl. Cut in butter until thoroughly blended. Roll into small balls. Fill a lightly greased baking sheet with balls placed 4 inches apart. Using a small glass, flatten balls. If glass sticks to dough, lightly butter bottom of glass. Bake for 10 to 12 minutes, until golden. Cool on wire racks.

Quick Tea Party Cookies

Makes 6 servings.

Peanut butter
12 vanilla wafer cookies
1 banana, sliced

Spread peanut butter on half of the wafers. Top each wafer with a slice of banana. Top with remaining wafers.

Teething Rings

Makes 18 pieces.

1 cup whole wheat flour (approximately)
2 tablespoons sifted soy flour
2 tablespoons non-instant dry milk
2 tablespoons raw wheat germ
1 egg, beaten
3 tablespoons honey
2 tablespoons vegetable oil

Preheat oven to 350°. Combine dry ingredients; mix lightly. Make a well in the center. Stir in liquid ingredients and mix thoroughly. Form dough into a ball and place on a well-floured surface. Knead until smooth. Divide dough and shape as desired. Place on lightly-greased baking sheets and bake for 10 minutes, or until golden. Store in a tightly covered container.

Fruit Salad Cones

Makes 6 servings.

1 8-ounce can chunk pineapple, drained
1 11-ounce can mandarin oranges, drained
¼ cup flaked coconut
1 cup colored miniature marshmallows
1 banana
1¼ cups nondairy whipped topping
6 flat-bottomed ice cream cones

Coarsely chop pineapple and oranges into small pieces. Combine pineapple, oranges, coconut and marshmallows in a mixing bowl. Cut banana into small pieces; add to bowl. Blend in whipped topping to coat all ingredients. Chill for 1 hour. Spoon into ice cream cones. If desired, garnish with whole maraschino cherries.

Fruit Salad Cone and Quick Tea Party Cookies, this page

Tuna Patties

Makes 6 servings.

- ½ cup milk
- ⅔ cup Grape Nuts cereal
- 2 tablespoons vegetable oil
- ½ cup minced onion
- 2 7-ounce cans water-packed tuna, drained and flaked
- 2 eggs, lightly beaten
  Salt and pepper to taste
- 1 teaspoon lemon juice

Combine milk and cereal in a small bowl. Set aside until cereal absorbs milk. Heat 1 tablespoon of the oil in a frying pan. Add onion and sauté until transparent. Add onion, tuna, eggs, seasonings and lemon juice to cereal. Mix well. Form into 12 patties. Heat remaining oil in the same pan the onions were sautéed in. Brown patties on both sides.

Shape cream cheese into small balls. Roll in granola and chill. Makes nutritious snacks for the toddler set.

Baby's Stroganoff

Makes 4 to 6 servings.

- 1 pound lean ground beef
- ½ cup minced onion
- 2 tablespoons whole wheat flour
- 2 cups beef broth
- ¾ cup unflavored yogurt

Sauté ground beef and onion until meat is browned and onion is tender. Stir in flour and cook for 2 minutes, stirring constantly. Slowly stir in beef broth. Bring to boil, stirring constantly. Reduce heat and simmer for about 30 minutes. Stir in yogurt and heat through without boiling. Serve over cooked noodles or rice.

Quick Vegetable Soup

- 1 16-ounce can tomatoes, chopped, with liquid
- 1 16-ounce can mixed vegetables, drained
- ½ cup macaroni
- ½ cup water
- 1 bay leaf, crushed
- ½ teaspoon garlic salt
  Salt and pepper, optional

Combine all ingredients in a medium saucepan. Cook over medium heat until macaroni is tender, stirring occasionally. Salt and pepper to taste.

Chicken Fricassee

Makes 4 to 5 servings.

- 3½ pounds chicken, cut into serving pieces
- ⅓ cup flour
- 1 teaspoon paprika
- ⅛ teaspoon black pepper
- 2 tablespoons butter or margarine
- 1 cup water
- ½ cup chopped onion
- 1 tablespoon minced chives
- ¼ cup chopped celery leaves
- 1 bay leaf
  Milk
  Whole wheat flour
  Salt, optional

Wash chicken and pat dry. Combine flour, paprika, and pepper in a bag. Add chicken pieces one at a time and shake bag to coat chicken. Melt margarine in a large frying pan. Brown chicken on all sides. Add water, onion, chives, celery leaves and bay leaf. Cover and simmer 1 hour or until chicken is tender. Remove chicken. Strain pan juices and add enough milk to make 3 cups. Combine enough whole wheat flour with leftover flour in shaking bag to make ⅓ cup. Pour a little of the milk-broth mixture into the flour and stir to make a thin paste. Slowly stir in remaining milk-broth mixture and return to frying pan. Cook until sauce is thick, stirring constantly. Discard bay leaf. Return chicken to pan. Remove baby's portion. Discard skin and bones. Chop or puree chicken along with a little of the sauce.

Chicken-Noodle Soup

Makes 3 to 4 servings.

- 3 cups chicken broth
- ½ cup cubed cooked chicken
- ¼ cup cubed cooked carrots
- ½ cup egg noodles

Place all ingredients in a saucepan and heat until noodles are tender. Remove baby's portion and blend as necessary.

Mini-Meat Loaves

Makes 4 servings.

- ¾ pound lean ground beef
- ¼ cup dry bread crumbs or oatmeal
- ¼ cup minced onion
- 1 egg
- ⅛ teaspoon ground sage
- ⅛ teaspoon ground thyme
- ⅛ teaspoon rosemary
- ¼ teaspoon minced parsley
- 1 tablespoon vegetable oil
- 1 tablespoon water

Combine the beef, bread crumbs, onion, egg and herbs; mix thoroughly. Divide the mixture into 8 portions and shape into loaves. Heat oil in a frying pan. Brown the meat loaves slowly on all sides. Add water to frying pan and cover tightly. Reduce heat and steam for 10 minutes. Turn off heat and let stand, covered, for 10 minutes.

FOR BABIES AND TODDLERS

Cream of Tomato Soup

Makes 4 servings.

- 1 tablespoon vegetable oil
- 1 rib celery, chopped
- ½ cup chopped onion
- 2 to 3 cups chopped tomatoes
- 1 tablespoon minced parsley
- 1 bay leaf
- 1 tablespoon cornstarch
- 1 cup milk
- ¼ cup grated Cheddar cheese

Heat oil in medium-sized, heavy frying pan. Sauté celery and onion until onion is tender. Add tomatoes, parsley and bay leaf and simmer, covered, 30 minutes, or until tomatoes are tender. Cool. Discard bay leaf. Place mixture in blender or food processor and purée. Strain, if desired. Return to pan; mix cornstarch with 2 tablespoons of the milk to form a paste. Stir into soup. Gradually stir in remaining milk, stirring until slightly thickened. Garnish with cheese.

Cheese Soufflé

Makes 4 servings.

- 3 eggs, separated
- ¼ pound Cheddar cheese
- ¼ cup milk
- ¼ teaspoon salt
  Dash cayenne pepper

Preheat oven to 325°. Beat egg whites until stiff peaks form. Melt cheese in a saucepan over hot water. Gradually add milk while stirring; stir until smooth. Add seasonings. In a small bowl, lightly mix egg yolks. Gradually stir egg yolks into cheese mixture. Remove from heat; set aside to cool. Gently fold in egg white until blended. Pour into a small, greased casserole. Bake for 20 minutes or until firm.

Sweet Potato Casserole

Makes 6 servings.

- 1½ pounds sweet potatoes
- ¼ cup margarine or butter
- 2 to 3 tablespoons milk
- 1 7-ounce can crushed pineapple, drained

Place sweet potatoes in a saucepan; cover with water. Bring to a boil, cover, and simmer 30 minutes, or until potatoes are fork tender. Cool and peel. Preheat oven to 350°. Combine potatoes, margarine and milk and beat until smooth. Stir in pineapple. Spoon into a 1-quart casserole. Bake 40 minutes or until heated through.

Potato and Liver Dinner

Makes 4 servings.

- 2 baking potatoes
  Margarine or butter
- 1 tablespoon hot milk
- ¼ cup grated Cheddar cheese
- 2 chicken livers, washed gently in milk

Preheat oven to 400°. Butter skins of potatoes and puncture each a few times with a fork. Bake 45 minutes to 1 hour or until tender. Slice each potato lengthwise keeping skins intact. Scoop out pulp and place in a bowl; mash. Stir in about 1 tablespoon margarine and the milk; beat until smooth. Add half of the cheese. Place half a chicken liver in the bottom of each potato skin. Cover with mashed potato. Sprinkle remaining cheese on top. Bake about 15 minutes or until liver is done. If tops brown before cooking time is up, cover with foil the last minutes of baking.

Veal Stew

Makes 4 servings.

- 1 pound veal stew meat
- ¼ cup whole wheat flour
- 2 tablespoons vegetable oil
- 3 cups tomato juice
- ⅛ teaspoon black pepper
- 1 cup cubed potatoes
- ½ cup sliced celery
- ½ cup chopped onion
- 2 tablespoons minced parsley
  Salt, optional

Dredge veal in flour. Heat oil in a heavy kettle or Dutch oven; brown meat on all sides. Add tomato juice and pepper. Cover and simmer 1 hour. Add vegetables and cook 30 minutes or until vegetables are tender. Remove baby's portion and chop or puree.

Baby's Beef Stew

Makes 4 to 5 servings.

- 2 tablespoons vegetable oil
- 1 pound lean beef stew meat
- 2 cups water or beef broth
- 2 teaspoons lemon juice
- 1 large clove garlic, minced
- 1 cup chopped onion
- 1 bay leaf
- ¼ teaspoon black pepper
- 5 carrots, sliced
- 2 to 3 potatoes, peeled and cubed
- 4 ribs celery

Heat oil in a soup kettle or Dutch oven. Brown meat on all sides. Add water. Reduce heat. Add lemon juice, garlic, onion, bay leaf and pepper. Cover and simmer until tender, about 2 hours. Add carrots, potatoes and celery. Cover and simmer until vegetables are tender. Remove baby's portion and chop or puree.

GLOSSARY

Bran The outer coating of the wheat kernel; high in B vitamins.

Carob A chocolate substitute made from the seeds of the St. John's plant. It is sold in powdered form in health food stores and supermarkets with specialty foods. Carob does not taste exactly like chocolate, but is a good substitute that is low in fat and caffeine free.

Graham flour Another name for whole grain or whole wheat flour. The best graham flour is stoneground and high in nutrients.

Noninstant powdered milk Contains more nutrients than instant powdered milk; usually more satisfactory in baking.

Nutritional yeast Another name for brewer's yeast. It is eaten raw. Provides protein and vitamin B complex.

Old-fashioned molasses Unsulphured, dark molasses.

Raw wheat germ The embryo or germ of the wheat kernel. Raw wheat germ is not toasted and therefore retains its high quality of protein and B vitamins.

Whole wheat flour Flour milled from the hard wheat grain, containing the endosperm, bran and germ.

Whole wheat pastry flour Milled from soft wheat; more finely ground than plain whole wheat flour.

SUBSTITUTIONS

If you wish to adapt some of your favorite recipes to make them more nutritious or if you don't have an ingredient called for, check this substitution list.

1 cup sour milk	= 1 cup milk plus 1 tablespoon vinegar or lemon juice (stir and let sit until it "clabbers")
	= 1 cup buttermilk
1 cup sour cream or buttermilk	= 1 cup yogurt
1 cup granulated sugar	= 1 cup or less honey in yeast breads; ⅞ cup honey in cookies and cakes; reduce liquid in recipe by 3 tablespoons (you have to experiment with honey)
1 cup all-purpose flour	= ⅞ cup whole wheat flour
	= ⅝ cup oat flour plus ⅜ cup rice flour
	= 1 cup unbleached flour
	= ⅔ cup whole wheat flour plus ⅓ cup raw wheat germ
	= ¾ cup whole wheat flour plus ¼ cup bran
	= ⅞ cup whole wheat flour plus 2 tablespoons soy flour (reduce baking temperature about 25° when adding soy flour)
⅓ cup cocoa	= ⅓ cup carob powder
1 tablespoon fresh herbs	= 1 teaspoon dried herbs
1 cup white, enriched, or converted rice	= 1 cup brown rice

INDEX

A
B
C
D
E
F
G
H
I
J
K
L
M